The Words We Use

Diarmaid Ó Muirithe

from his Irish Times *column*

FOUR COURTS PRESS

The Words We Use

By the same author
A Dictionary of Anglo-Irish: Words and Phrases from Gaelic

(*with T.P. Dolan*)
The Dialect of Forth and Bargy

The Words We Use

Diarmaid Ó Muirithe

FOUR COURTS PRESS

Set in 10 on 12 point Bembo
and published by
FOUR COURTS PRESS LTD
Kill Lane, Blackrock, Co. Dublin, Ireland
and in North America by
FOUR COURTS PRESS LTD
c/o ISBS, 5804 NE Hassalo Street, Portland, OR 97213.

A catalogue record for this title
is available from the British Library.

ISBN 1-85182-220-8

Printed in Ireland
by Colour Books Ltd, Dublin.

For Barry, Rita and Lara,
and for Maurice Manning

ACKNOWLEDGMENT

These articles are reproduced from the *Irish Times*,
by kind permission of the Editor.

Contents

9 Skaith and a Piper's Finger
  Jails, Andremartins, Headache
10 Proverbs
11 Moither, Ducky
12 Dingley-cooch and Other
  Matters
13 Stugue and Tig
14 Haar, and Some Tipperary
  Words
15 Piping Hot, Merra, Nivels and
  Snivels
16 Smirk and Ladoose
  Pladdy, Greth and Words of
  Endearment
17 Drink and Fushion
18 Sorra Hate
19 Yankee, Scopse and Saraft
20 Jorum, Cronebane, Peaked
21 No Daw
22 Beyond the Pale, and Some
  Celtic Words
23 Arseward, Ballyragged,
  Amplush
24 Forlorn Hope
25 Swail and Shucks!
  Vareen, Dunt, Camalough
26 Stour, Greip
27 Tugging the Katshee and
  Other Matters
28 Slink, Grush and Gruff
29 Smoor, Smurdikeld and
  Smoorich
30 Anathema
  Some Handlin'
31 Overright, Minikin, Paddle
  and Pill
32 County Dublin Invective
33 Giglet and Strone
34 Polthogue, Sorra and Smit
35 Rocket, Kitchen, Lambaste

36 Garble, Astonish
37 Wha' cheer, boy?
  Skelp, Woar, Skip
38 Disguised and Gawky
39 Whist!
40 Words from County Louth
41 The New Testament in Scots
42 Ayrshire Words for Mayhem
43 Fockles and Brawse
44 Birds
45 Panaydee, Wisha!
46 Strap and Fiasco
  Husbands and Other Matters
47 Old Dublin Words
48 Bonefires and Banjaxed
49 Paddyisms?
50 Moll Doyle
51 Queens and Queans
  Middlebrows and Musebrows
52 Fortnail, Shool, and a Tudor
  Survival
53 Mismanners and Other 'Mis'
  Words
54 Pregnant Pauses
55 Cards and Card-playing Terms
  Molly Bloom's Budget
56 Latchikoes and Policasters
57 Donegal Words
58 Norse Words from the
  South-East
59 Can-can
  Scalteen
60 John Florio and His Dictionary
61 Northern Words
62 False Etymologies
63 Country Words
64 Really Boss, Balderdash
65 Flamenco, Gringo and Swift's
  Crux
  Comfort and Good Cheer

66 Rockers, Rakes and Locks
67 Dying Words?
68 More Birds
69 Barmy
70 Liverpool English
71 Box-fast and Sleaving Ropes
72 H.C. Hart
   Partridge
73 Homer in Scots
74 Pet
75 Gigs and Jigs
76 Shall and Will
77 Kitty, Glar, Glit, Dailigone
78 Pleach and Plash, Sally and
   Willow
79 Influence
80 Dusk
81 Crack
   More Crack
82 The Twangman
83 Poppets and Moppets
84 Scantlin and Dick Grace
85 Cards
86 Gurriers
87 The Glenswilly Decree
88 Kibosh
   Americanisms
89 Early American Words
90 Ballyhoo
91 Tuam Schoolboy Slang
92 You Don't Say
93 Chimneys
   Bailey's Dictionary
94 Jackson
95 Mockt
96 Political Correctness or Plain
   Lunacy
97 Postures
98 Culinary Words
   Borrowings
99 Shakespeare and the Computer
100 Brass Monkeys

101 A Bee in His Bonnet
102 Earwigs and Other Creatures
103 Tell It to the Marines
   My Country, Right or Wrong
104 Love and Deuce, Hijack
105 Slang
106 Punnin, Hessians and Naked
   Truth
107 Me Oul Segosha
108 Some Phrases and a Shambles
109 In Search of Purity
110 Newfoundland English
111 Clips and Rhyming Doublets
   Cockney Slang
112 Shelta
113 Blowens
114 Parlyaree
115 Racist Terms
116 Mots and Sooty Blowens
117 Dublin Slang from 1788
   Jacks and Loo
118 Skoolyunes and Snobs
119 It's and Its
120 Brats and the Waterford
   Uvular R
121 Phil Wall's Words
   Kim-Kam
123 Remembering Prayers
   Omlish and Alfratch
124 By Hook or by Crook
125 Cummer
126 That's Cat, Precious
   Archbishop Trench
127 Waur and Trance
128 Tipperary Words
129 Moral and Some Donegal
   Words
130 All My Eye
131 Egg on
   Fridgies and Slammicks
132 Nominy
133 Jimp and Traipse

Skaith and a Piper's Finger

Have you heard the Strollers sing? You have had plenty of time to do so, for they have been in existence since before the Fenian rising (1867). They are a musical/dining club, based in Rathgar and their honorary secretary, Mr Maurice McDonough, has written to me to enquire about a word in one of their favourite songs, *If Doughty Deeds*, attributed (at least the words are) to a Scot called Graham of Gartmore who flourished in the 18th century. In it the man says to his loved one: 'Nae maiden lays her skaith to me, I never loved but you.' What, the Strollers ask, is her *skaith*?

'Nor fear wound or scath from hand of mine,' wrote the Co. Down man, Savage-Armstrong, in his *Ballads* of 1901. *Scath/scaith/scathe* meant injury, damage, hurt, loss. 'To have gotten skaith' is glossed as 'to have been bewitched' by a Scotsman at the end of the last century: 'Thus men or cattle are said to have gotten scaith when it is believed that the disease which affects them proceeds from preternatural influence.' This is what our friend in the song is going on about: he is telling his lover that no other woman has bewitched him.

The word is from Old English *sceatha*, related to Old Norse *skathi* and the Old Saxon *scatho*. It is rare now, but still to be found in rural places from John of Groats to Devon and Somerset and, I shouldn't be surprised, north of Ballymena and in Co. Down. Of course, its cousin, *scathing*, is still alive and kicking everywhere.

Mary Lavelle, Australian-born if not -bred, wrote from Melbourne to ask if I've heard an expression used by her mother, who came from the country of Mayo—*lyrakeen peebora*. She knows that it is Irish, but has never found out what it meant. Her mother used to say: 'That fellow is about as useful as a lyrakeen peebora.' It was applied to useless footballers, politicians—and, on occasions, husbands. 'I hope it's not anything obscene,' she adds, with admirable concern for my innocence.

Mary's expression is a transmutation of *laidhricín piobaire*, a piper's little finger; I'm given to understand that the *laidhricín/lyrakeen* is *not* used in playing the uileann pipes. Twenty years ago, that man of words, Fr Leon Ó Moracháin, recorded the phrase in Louisburgh, near Clew Bay. I wonder if it is still in the west, in either Irish or Irish English.

Jails, Andremartins, Headache

I haven't seen my old friend, Mrs Wall, who used to park her horse-drawn caravan close to where I live in Co. Wicklow, for quite a while. She would, undoubtedly, be able to answer a question asked by Ann O'Mahony, of Douglas, Cork, about the word *goal*—not the net into which the Irish soccer team has, of late, been unable to propel the ball (that's from Middle English *gol*, boundary), but a word meaning jail, prison. Ann has heard *goal* used by a travelling man; she is sure the word she heard isn't *gaol*. Is *goal* a Shelta word, she wonders?

In the absence of Mrs Wall, who speaks Shelta to her daughter, I'm afraid I can't answer. But this I know: the word *goal* was common in south-east Ireland in the last century. Patrick Kennedy has it in *The Banks of the Boro* (Wexford, 1867)—'Come pay for the whole, Or else you'll be the first man in the goal.' Back in 1753 we find 'For the Goal and the Marchalsea' in a Scottish parish account book; and in a little book called *Tales*, written by a Kentish man in 1790, we find 'Quorum wigs upon my soul, Mind me, says Snap-crust, of a goal.'

Goal is certainly not a misreading, or a mispronunciation of *gaol*. Both words are of equal age, from Old French *jaiole*, a cage, from Latin *cavea*, enclosure.

As I watched the great New Zealand fly-half, Andrew Mehrtens in action recently, I was reminded of a word I have heard many times and whose origin is a mystery to me—*andremartins*. It means silly tricks, nonsensical behaviour. P.J. McCall, who was a valued contributor to the English Dialect Dictionary, said the word was common all over Leinster, including Dublin city, in his time (circa 1890). He gave an example of its use: 'Don't be goin' on with your andramartins.' Does anybody know the origin of this word?

Mary Murphy from Carlow wants to know if I've ever seen a *headache*. Indeed I have, Mary. The *headache* is the common red poppy, and in the last century it was regarded as particularly obnoxious to the females of south Leinster, 'the more so to unmarried young women, who have a horror of touching or being touched by them', according the English Dialect Dictionary, which neglected to explain why this was so. Is it still true of the young ladies of Carlow, Mary? John Clare in *The Shepherd's Calendar* (1827) has 'Corn-poppies that in crimson dwell. Call'd headaches from their sickly smell.' Look out for them in the cornfields of July.

Proverbs

Today, not words but Irish proverbs, and for a reason. No doubt many of my readers will have had a surfeit of them from their schooldays when it was deemed advantageous to lace essays with them. Never mind. Read on.

T.F. O'Rahilly has this one in his *Miscellany of Irish Proverbs*: Ní hí an bhreáthacht a chuireann an corcán ar fiuchadh—*Beauty never made the pot boil*. One from Ulster, written down by Robert MacAdam in 1861: Is í an dias is troime is ísle a chromas a ceann—*The heaviest ear of corn hangs its head the lowest.* A beautiful metaphor, implying that the man who has the most learning should be the most modest. One from our schooldays: Is fear rith maith ná drochsheasamh—*A good run is better than a bad stand.* And how about this gem of political correctness from O'Rahilly and Munster: Bean, muc, is miúil, an triúr is deacra a mhúineadh—*Three without rule, a pig, a woman, and a mule.*

The *Gaelic Journal* of 1906 has: Ding den leamhán a scoilteann í féin—*A wedge of elm to split the elm.* A rogue to catch a rogue, a thief to catch a thief, if you like. Another one from Munster: Ceangail leis an lom agus ceanglóidh an lom leat—*Be bare with the soil and the soil will be bare with you.* Henry Morris collected this in Ulster: Na trí ní is súgaí amuigh, pisín cait, meannán gabhair agus baintreach óg mná—*The three merriest things under the sun, a cat's kitten, a goat's kid, and a young widow.* And here's another one from Morris from Farney: Is uaigneach an níochán nach mbionn léine ann—*It's a lonesome washing that has not a man's shirt in it.*

Now the reason I give these today is to draw your attention to the translations given in italics. These are not mine, nor are they the work of the collectors. They were collected as I have given them here in the middle of this century in North Carolina, and published by B.J. Whiting of Harvard in the *Journal of Celtic Studies* 1, 1949–50; the homely wisdom of those destitute people who left this country a century and a half ago in what they, with astonishing understatement, called an *droch shaol*, the bad times.

Moither, Ducky

The late Tony Galento, the boxer, once achieved fleeting fame of a kind when, in answer to a question as to what he thought of William Shakespeare, he replied that he could moider de bum. Jane Shawe from Belfast wrote asking about a different *moider*, also spelled *moither* and *moydher*, a word common enough in the Antrim of her youth, she tells me. *Moither* (the most common Irish spelling) means to confuse, perplex, bewilder; to worry, bother, fatigue.

Moither was used frequently in 19th century Irish literature. 'I dhramed it the night asleep and awake till I was fairly moithered in me head,' wrote Jane Barlow in *Lisconnel* (1895). 'This living' air is moithered wi' the bumming o' the bees,' wrote Moira O'Neill in her *Songs of the Glens of Antrim*, in 1900. A.D. Simmons, too, has it in his glossary of Armagh and south Donegal English (1890). It is common in Scotland and in the northern and midland counties of England. 'Of uncertain origin', the dictionaries say. The first time it was seen in print was in a book called *Wit of a Woman*, published in 1705.

This contains the sentence, 'I've been strangely moyder'd e're sin 'bout this same news o' the French king.' It is from Early Irish, *modarda*, confused.

Mary Kelleher from Macroom wants to know where the word *puntham* comes from. She has heard the word used by mountainy men, she says, to describe a woman. She doesn't know whether the word is derogatory or not. There is an Irish word *puntam*, and Father Dinneen got it in Ballyvourney. It means, he says, a lively person, especially a woman of low stature. He speculated that is a borrowing from English. I'm not sure whether a woman would be pleased to be called a bantam, in any language.

But what about being called ducky? A lady from Dalkey tells me that she was offended twice recently in my own dear native Wexford by old fellows in a pub who said things like 'Hello, ducky', to her. I'm no chicken, she says, but I don't like being compared to a duck. That term of endearment *ducky*, has nothing to do with ducks, Margaret. It is from the Norse *dokka*, a word that has a counterpart in the modern Danish *dukke*. It means a doll. Happier?

Dingley-cooch and Other Matters

The man in the Dublin department store was getting a wee bit annoyed with the missus. He had a rich northern accent. What he said to herself interested me: 'I'm not goin' to stond here all day listenin' to you cobblin.' To *cobble* means to bargain, to haggle. I knew the word from the vocabulary of northern horse dealers. It is very old: it comes from the Old Norse *kaupa*, to buy.

Risteard de Róiste of Duncormack, Co. Wexford, wrote to tell me of a word in common use in his native place—*stife*. It means, fumes, smoky atmosphere. This word is common in the mining towns of the neighbouring island, but I've never come across it in Ireland, other than in Mr de Róiste's native district. Across the water it is applied especially to the fumes and foul air of a mine. Hence they also have *stifeness*, closeness of the atmosphere; *stifing*, ppl. adj. choking from fumes; and *stifey*, adj., oppressive, causing difficulty in breathing. All these words, confined now to the mining districts of Britain, are of course, related to *stifle* and *stifling*, from Old English *stuflen*, itself probably from Old French *estouffer*, to smother.

Mary Doyle of Carlow wants to know where the word *gam*, a leg, comes from. *Gam* is usually classified as being Irish, but it was in English cant in the 18th century. In Parker's *Life's Painter* (1781) it is explained that 'If a man has bow legs, he has queer gams, gams being cant for legs.' *Gam* has a long pedigree: it came to us from the Norman French, *gambe*, a leg. Compare French *jambe*.

As I was trawling through some Ulster glossaries the other day I came upon the expressions *Dingley-cooch* and *Dinglety-cootch*. 'He's gone to Dingley-cootch' means he's done something discreditable, according to Patterson (Antrim); and to 'send a man to Dinglety-cootch' means to send him to Coventry. A very common expression in the north, according the English Dialect Dictionary. From the Kerry town Daingean Uí Chúis, anglicised Dingle, 'from the remoteness and inaccessibility of that place,' the English Dialect Dictionary explains. No comment.

Finally, thanks to Mrs A. Anderson of Ballymena for the nice letter and for the expression, 'That's right, hang the kelp,' said to a child whose lower lip is drooping in a sulk. The *kelp* was the iron hook on which pots were hung over the open fire. A great survival, it is from Old Norse *kjelp*, the handle of a pot.

Stugue and Tig

Joseph Wright was a conscientious and meticulous editor, and his six-volume dictionary of dialect words for Oxford is a wonderful treasury. He and his fellow workers sometimes trod on dangerous ground when dealing with words collected in Ireland, and I notice that they were at a loss concerning a word still in use in the south-east, both as a noun and a verb. The word is *stugue*. Somebody who had read Patrick Kennedy's books had sent Wright the word, and he promptly consigned it to a Supplement at the back of the final volume, which contained words which were kept back, 'because the authority for many of these words is unsatisfactory.'

In *The Banks of the Boro* (1876) Kennedy has: 'He began to think that his inside would be all gone, and that he'd fall in a stugue on one of the big diamond-shaped flags of the floor.' In *Evenings in the Duffrey* (1869) he uses the word as a verb: 'To beg some good Christian to give him a drink of could wather, or he'd stugue up.' Meaning unknown, says Wright. Stugue is Irish *stua*, *stuag* in the older language. It means an arch, an arc. I myself have heard 'He made a stugue of him with he handle of the hurl.' I daren't say where.

A reader from Sligo wrote concerning the name of the children's game, *tig*. Does it come from the Irish? she asks.

Not at all. And apart from being the name of a game played by kids all over Britain and Ireland it has other interesting meanings. 'Young people are said to be tigging when sporting with gentle touches or patting each other,' wrote a Scots correspondent to Wright, adding intriguingly, 'it properly applies to those of different sexes.' To tig also means 'to make love to; to have intercourse with, either friendly or criminal', according to another Scots source.

The game of tig and the other games mentioned above are also known as *tick*. Shakespeare would have known the children's game as *tick-and-no-den*; and Burns the other games as *ticken and tannin*.

So what's the origin of *tig/tick*? It came from the Dutch sailors who had a go at making a stugue of the English fleet long ago (compare the East Frisian *tikken*, to touch lightly); and it is thought that they used the word only in relation to matters of an amorous nature. Well, you know what sailors are.

Haar, and Some Tipperary Words

The recent spell of glorious weather was caused, I was informed by a Wicklowman who likes to boast of his expertise in matters meteorological, 'by some class of an antichrist cyclin' around Ireland'. Miss Cusack of the Met Service certainly got it right on television. Not a cloud in the sky for a week, she promised, except for a *haar* over the eastern coast of southern Scotland and northern England. She had the word written on her weather map; I hadn't heard it in years. It means a cold sea-mist, fog, or an easterly onshore wind. Of Dutch origin. Compare Middle Dutch *hare*, a cold wind, and Dutch dialect *harig*, mist.

Sailors and trawlermen have a few sayings about the *haar*. One is 'a northern *haar* brings fine weather from afar'. That's a Yorkshire one. I heard the word from my Wexford grandmother, whose people were seafarers.

A lady from Cashel sent me some very interesting words used by her grandfather, she tells me, when the world was a biteen younger. One was *freeheen*. This was the name given to the men and women from the bogs who sold loads of turf in Cashel and Thurles. These people arrived in town at daybreak, deposited their loads of turf and carefully rebuilt them in small stacks, containing perhaps half a ton. *Freeheen* was a slightly insulting term, she says, like culchie, and never used to a turf-seller's face on account of their skill with the ash-plant.

Freeheen is from Irish *fraoch*, heather. But the turf-sellers got the name, not because they lived in the bog, but because they bound the tops of their carefully built loads with decorative bands of heather. These, my informant tells me, were the freeheens (*fraoichíní*).

Another interesting word is *allagashtees*. These were gewgaws, or tawdry items of jewellery or clothing. 'You're surely not going to wear them allagashtees to Mass, are you?', her granny used to say to the young miss, who tells me candidly that she hasn't a clue where the word comes from. I can reply with equal candour that neither do I. Perhaps some reader may be able to solve this problem for us.

Another of my correspondent's words is *moonshlay*, emphasis on the second syllable, a flash flood in the river, beloved of anglers, if not of farmers in low-lying lands. This is Irish, *maidhm sléibhe*, a mountain burst or eruption. Nothing to worry about while yer man is cycling around Ireland.

Piping Hot, Merra, Nivels and Snivels

Mary O'Brien writing from Limerick, wants to know what the origin of the phrase *piping hot* is; why *piping*?

The phrase is in colloquial use wherever English is spoken. You'll find it in the street cries of 19th-century England. Mutton pies were sold to the cry of 'Piping hot, smoking hot! Pies, pies, all hot, all hot!' in Dickens' London. But the phrase is much older. Chaucer has it in the *Canterbury Tales*: 'And wafres, pyping hote out of the glede.' But to answer the Limerick lady's question, the only explanation I can think of is that piping hot means, so hot as to hiss; from Old English verb *pipian*, ultimately from Latin *pipare*, to chirp.

From Sligo comes a query as to the word *merra*. 'The place do be full of half-naked Dutch and Swedish merras in the Summer,' said a local man to my correspondent, a Dutchwoman herself. Her enquiry as to the meaning of *merra* brought a smile and the helpful answer, 'Ah, sure, you know yourself!' 'Is *merra* a naughty word?' I am asked.

No. Yeats refers to one in his *Folktales* (1888). He spells the word *merrow*, as does Lawless in *Grania* (1892): 'My grandfather saw one once on the head of a merrow by the Glassan rock.' Crofton Croker in his *Legends* (1862) has *merrow* from Killarney: 'Dick guessed at once that she was a merrow.' *Merra/merrow* is a mermaid. The word is from the Irish *murúch*.

A word I haven't heard in ages was sent to me by Mary Power from Ferrybank in south Kilkenny, just across the river from Waterford city. The word is *nivel*. The late Donal Foley had it, and so had my Wexford grandmother. *Nivel* means to turn up the nose in disdain; to make a face as children do at the sight of food they don't want to eat.

This is a very old word. It is in *Piers Plowman*: 'Thenne a-waked Wrathe with to white eyen, With a *nyuylynge* nose nyppyung hus lyppes.' It is a variant of the Norman dialect word *nifler*, 'to sniff noisely, like a dog', an old glossary tells me.

Is *nivel* related to *snivel*? Very distantly, perhaps. *Snivel* is from Middle English *snevelen*, from Old English *synflung*, and *snofl*, mucus. But then *snofl* is related to Old Norse *snoppa*, the nose, which kids turn up when nivveling at being served food they don't like. But you can nivel without a snivel. Oh dear! It's a complicated world, this world of words.

Smirk and Ladoose

Jean Randall from Belfast asks what the origin of *smirk* is. She has a reason for so asking; her mother, who came from Galloway, knew *smirk*, noun, as a pleasant smile, and as a verb, to look pleasantly. 'Can this be the same word as we find in the standard dictionaries?' she asks: '*smirk*, noun, a smile expressing scorn or smugness rather than pleasure, and *smirk*, verb, to smile in a sneering fashion.

Ultimately, both types of smirk comes from Sanskrit, *smera*, smiling, and *smáyate*, smiles. From these we get Old English *smearcian*, related to Old High German *smieron*, smile. But we also have the Old English *smerian*, laugh at. It would seem that their child, *smirk*, meant at first simply a pleasant laugh. The Scots have kept that meaning (so have some of the older people in Donegal and Antrim) while the rest of us have chosen to see in the word a certain derisive quality. 'With perfect joy the body smirks, An' fain would fall a laughing,' wrote a poet from Mrs R's mother's Galloway, where they also had *smirker*, noun, one who smiles pleasantly, and the adjective *smirky*, smiling. 'I will bless and I will kiss thy bonny face, my smirky lass' said a swain in *The Shepherd's Wedding* (1789).

But there's another *smirk*, found in Scotland and in Ulster. It means to strike or slap, and in particular to get the creases out of linen. As a noun it also means a kiss. Grant, a good dialect poet, has in his *Lays* (1884): 'Most met the lads wi' ready mou's, An' never gae a thraw, Althou', instead o' ae bit smirk, They happened to get twa.'

There is also the lovely *smirkle* and *smirkling*, words I heard in the Rosses in the Sixties. The old Meenbanad woman who used them told me that to smirkle meant to giggle. Old words, these. The Scots poet Montgomerie used *smirkling* back in 1597: 'Experience then smyrkling smyled.' Sparkling words. Are they still alive in Ireland, I wonder?

Mary O'Callaghan from Cork's Blackrock wants to know where *ladoose* comes from. Her west Cork grandfather used to put a stop to conversation by saying, 'ah ladoose!' This is Irish *ladús*, which Dinneen defines as 'foolish talk, impertinence, nonsense'. In Ballyvourney it meant mildly flirtatious, erotic talk. 'She's no angel, that one, to judge from the ladús she had with an old dog like myself', said a young fellow of 80, who happened to be my uncle, to me once. And then, smyrkling, he smyled. (See also p. 24 below.)

Pladdy, Greth and Words of Endearment

The problem of the Co. Down word *pladdy*, a submerged rock, which has been bothering Mr John Wilde Crosbie, has, I feel pretty sure, been solved by Prof. Bö Almqvist of UCD. He suggests the Norse *floeði*, originally in a compound such as *floeðisker*, a skerry which is flooded at high water.

Ann Boyle, writing from London, tells me that she was born near Ardara, Co. Donegal. A word in common use there was *greth*; she wants to know a little of its history. It intrigues her, she says, because it meant a variety of things: furniture, equipment, household bits-and-pieces; clothes, dress; the trappings of a horse.

The word is also spelled *graith* in various parts of Scotland and England. It was used extensively in the literature of Scotland since about 1200, and it is found as far south as Pembrokeshire today. I haven't heard it used as a verb in the north of Ireland, but you'll hear 'graith the table' in Yorkshire.

Burns has *graith*, noun, in *Tam Sampson*, a gentleman he saw 'in shootin' graith adorn'd'. And as for *greth/graith*, meaning a horse's harness, Scott, in *Midlothian*, has 'horse-graith an' harnessing'. The word is of Scandinavian origin; there is the Old Norse *greiða*, to arrange, make ready, and *greiði*, arrangement, ordering.

Mrs J. H. from south Tipperary sent me a nice letter in the course of which she complains that this wretched PC nonsense has the world of the heart, as she calls it, ruined. 'In my young days, a long time ago now, many's the young fellow told me that I was (a) a smashin' *pustogue* (b) a lovely little pony (c) a cuddly *pishkin*. Tell me, and tell me no more, where do *pishkin* and *pustogue* come from? I know what a pony is.'

Pishkin is Irish *piscín*, a kitten. *Pustogue* is Irish *pustóg*, a woman with a sexy pout. The word is not in the dictionaries, but it has been recorded in Kilkenny and Carlow. I once heard it applied to La Bardot in Graigue-namanagh. *Pus* means mouth.

To be called a *pony* has been, for centuries past, considered a compliment by Munster women. The Augustinian Jacobite poet, Liam Inglis, used the word nearly 250 years ago to describe the beautiful young woman, Ireland: *Póiní an Leasa*: the pony of the fairy fort.

Robert Sharpe tells me that in the Glens of Antrim a pretty girl is called a *shelty* (from *Shetland*). Another pony. Another compliment.

Drink and Fushion

'When I first went to school in Belfast I was told that I wouldn't be of much use to the rugby team as I was a *drink*. On enquiry, I was told that a drink was a person grown too tall for his age, and consequently weak of limb and frame. The word was not meant to be insulting, unlike the phrase "a drink of water", meaning a milksop, which was commonly used in my home town

of Bangor. Why *drink*, tell me? And are the word and the phrase related?'
So writes John Bell.

I've heard 'a drink of water' in the south; but this is, I think, a phrase of
modern origin, and unrelated to the drink you were called in school, Mr
Bell. Since this word *drink* has not travelled any great distance south, I assume
it came to Ulster from Scotland. 'He's gotten a lang drink o' a wife' was
recorded in Perthshire, while 'Stair has grown up into a great lang drink an''
would fankle if he fell' was overheard in Burns' country. (To *fankle* means
to twist, knot, entangle, by the way.) *Drink* comes from the Old Norse *drengr*,
a young married man. You may compare the modern Norwegian dialect
word *drenghall*, an unmarried man.

Mrs J. Scott who lives in or near Warrenpoint, sent me the word *fushion* to
try me during the penitential season. 'My mother used it often,' she tells me.
'It means nourishment. She would say to us: 'Eat up. There's great fushion
in that.' Where does the word come from?'

Another fine Ulster (and Scots) word this. I had the devil's own trouble
tracking it down because it is spelled *foison* in the dialect dictionaries in
deference to its origin. It can mean (a) plenty, abundance, especially with
reference to the harvest. 'Man intends, God foizon sends' is an old Sussex
saying. (b) Nourishing power, hence nourishment. (c) Sap, juices.

There is also the good word *fushionless*—'applied to meal of flour which
has been damaged; insipid or innutritious, as applied to fodder of inferior
quality', according to the *Ballymena Observer* (1892). 'I'm for whisky still.
Nane o' your fushionless, cauld wish—wash for me,' wrote a great rhymer
with a fondness for John Barleycorn.

Fushion in all its spellings came to Scotland and Ulster from France: *foison*
is 'store, plenty, abundance' according to Cotgrave's great 17th-century
dictionary; and *foison, fuzzen* or *fusen* means 'nourishment, natural juyce',
according to that treasury of country words, Worlidge's *Dictionarium rusticum*
of 1681.

Sorra Hate

Mr Dan Swift of Glenbrook Park, Rathfarnham, tells me that he is a native
of the fair county of Westmeath. He wants to know the origin of the word
hate, used in his native place as follows:

Q   Was there much wrong with him after the accident?
A   Sorra hate.
Q   How was he after the accident?
A   Not a hate wrong with him.

Hate, also found as *hait*, should, I suppose, be spelled *hate* or *haet*. The noun means 'a whit, the smallest thing that can be conceived: generally negative, as Mr Swift points out. It started life in such phrases as *deil haet* (the devil have it), or *fien haet*, (the fiend have it) in Scotland. This deprecatory expression became a very strong negative, the equivalent of devil a bit, i.e. not a bit. Hence *haet*, with an ordinary negative, as Mr Swift's *sorra hate* and *not a hate*, came to be understood as equivalent to 'whit, atom', according to the English Dialect Dictionary. I wonder has it been recorded even further south than Co. Westmeath?

Margaret Whitty is a Wexford woman who now lives in Zimbabwe, and she wrote to ask if I had ever heard the word *haddick* meaning a discarded friend, a jilted lover, anybody left on the empty shore, as the saying goes. Many's the time have I heard it south of the road that runs between Ross and Wexford town; I had written it down as *haddock*. Haddocks in Wexford, and in Wexford alone, according to the English Dialect Dictionary, are imperfectly threshed heads of corn, discarded after winnowing; the word more often than not, is used figuratively. *Haddock/haddick* is a variant of *hattock*, a word not used in Wexford.

Diarmuid Breathnach from Bray sent me a Co. Tipperary word that has me puzzled. The word is *moodavoul*; a friend of his has also heard *moodavow*. A *moodavoul* or *moodavow* is the silent type who sits alone in country pubs listening to private conversations. I wonder where this strange word came from?

I am glad to be able to Sarah Craig where her Co. Down grandfather's interjection *Palm!* originated. This is what the good man used to shout when he played a winning trump card. It was originally *Pam*, the King of clubs, the big trump in the game of Loo, mentioned by Pope in the *Rape of the Lock*. 'Ev'n mighty Pam that Kings and Queens o'erthrew. And mow'd down enemies in the fights of lu.' From *Pamphile*, the *Knave* of Clubs in an old French card game.

Yankee, Scopse and Saraft

Helen Wall from Limerick and Brian Gaffney from Dublin's Clontarf would like to know what the true origin of *Yankee* is. Both have heard, or read, that it is an American Indian mispronunciation of the word *English*.

The word has a more interesting etymology, if we are to believe the great American dictionaries, which claim that the word is ultimately from the Dutch *Jan Kees*, a dialectal variant of *Jan Kaas* (literally) John Cheese, a nickname for Dutch and English settlers. The -*s* was taken in English as a plural ending.

Michael Flynn of Bawndaw, Gracedieu, Waterford, wrote to ask about the word *sconse*, the top of the head. 'I have only heard this word used by my mother and her relatives in such phrases as "Get your sconse into that sink", at hair-washing time,' he says, but adds that in Ballybricken he has heard *skonks*.

This is an old word, and most dictionaries describe it as either obsolete or archaic. Collins says that it dates from the 16th century, and that it is probably a jocular use of Old French *esconse*, a hiding place, a lantern; or from the Late Latin *sconsa*, from Latin *absconsa*, dark lantern. On the other hand, the excellent *American World Book Dictionary* says the ultimate origin of sconse, the head, may be the Dutch *schans*, brushwood used as a protective screen. Washington Irving has 'Peter Stuyvesant dealt him a twack over the sconse with his wooden leg.' Well done, Waterford, for keeping your word.

Mary Brennan of Wellington Lane, Dublin, has been reading a novel called *Waiting*, by Gerald O'Donovan (1914). In it she found a word that has intrigued her—*Saraft*. An eligible east Galway bachelor is enjoying the Hallow E'en festivities. One of the nuts placed by some girl in the embers has popped out towards him, signifying that she is to be his one day, and he says: 'I'm afeared I'm done for this Saraft. . . . There's no going back on a nut.'

Saraft is a variant of *Shraft*, Shrovetide. It is a word found only in Ireland, as far as I know. 'Will you have my coat made agin Shraft?' wrote Carleton in *Traits and Stories of the Irish Peasantry*. In Wexford the word was *Sraft*. 'I was in Iniscorfy, you see, on Sraft Tuesday,' wrote Patrick Kennedy in *The Banks of the Boro* in 1867. In Galway they added a vowel to make *Saraft*. Is the word still in use there, I wonder? It still is in parts of Wexford. We're a conservative lot.

Jorum, Cronebane, Peaked

The origin of the dialect word *jorum*, a drink, is troubling Mr G. Hewson of Belfast. He has heard the word often in Scotland and in England as well as in Ireland, and he wonders whether a friend of his is correct in saying that the word is from the Irish *deor*, a tear, a drop of liquid.

Not a bit of it. Formerly a *jorum* meant a large jug or pitcher; it also meant the contents of such a vessel. You'll find the word frequently used in the literature of the 18th and 19th centuries in Scotland and England. Sand's *Poems* of 1833 has the lines: 'Thae twa chief o' a' the quorum/That cam' that night to hae a jorum.' But the word came, not from *deor*, but from the proper name *Joram*, in allusion to that gentleman's connection with 'vessels of silver, and vessels of gold, and vessels of brass' in the Second Book of Samuel. *Jeroboam* is a like derivation from a personal name found in Scripture.

A woman who wants to remain anonymous wants to know the origin of a word she read in one of the Banim brothers novels, something wasn't worth a *cronebane*, a coin of some kind. Is it from the Irish *coróin bhán*, a silver or white crown, she wonders. No. The *cronebane* was a halfpenny copper token used by Associated Irish Mines in the 1790s. By the Banims' time it wouldn't have been worth much, I suppose. The coppermines were at a place called Conebane, in Co. Wicklow.

'When we were children', writes Mary O'Reilly from Swords 'my mother might say, "you should rest, you're looking peaked". By this she meant washed-out looking, or indeed, sick. I haven't heard the word in years.'

The English Dialect Dictionary didn't record it anywhere in Ireland, but it is to be found in the northern counties. It is common across the water, and in America. Mrs Gaskell has it in *Sylvia* (1863): 'Thou'rt looking as peaked and pined as a Methody preacher after a love-feast.' And from Hampshire an informant gave the great dictionary: 'She do look very peakish of late', a construction that may surprise many Irish people, incidentally.

The origin of *peak* in this sense is unknown. Who, then, was the first to use it in literature? You'll remember 'Weary se'nnights nine times nine/ Shall he dwindle, peak, and pine' from *Macbeth*. Ah dear! When I think that he's out of favour in Marlboro Street I do be peakish myself—as they might say in Hugginstown, or Hampshire.

No Daw

'All over Ireland I've heard people use the expression, 'He/she is no daw.' What exactly is a daw? I know that it means a foolish person. Could the word be related to the dialect word for the curse of chimneysweeps, *corvus monedula*, the jackdaw? The questions come from Monica Kenny (I think it is) of Sutton, Co. Dublin.

Daw is related to the Old High German word *taha*, and the English Dialect Dictionary suggests that from this daw, the bird, we got daw, an idle, chattering person; a lazy good-for-nothing, a sluggard; a slattern; a fool. 'What better is the house that the daw rises early in the morning?' is spoken often by mistresses to their maids when they have been up early, and done little work', according to Kelly's *Proverbs*, a famous Scottish collection published in 1721. 'An only dochter (daughter) is either a deil or a daw', is another proverb, this time from Henderson's collection of 1832. 'What's good o' listenin' to a daw like that? When I fall oot it's wi' men no' wi' maggits', was recorded in southern Scotland some years later. From Antrim, that treasury of Ulster Scots words, The *Ballymena Observer* (1892), has 'A' days bra and on Sundays a daw'.

I have never heard the three words given by the English Dialect Diction-ary as offshoots of daw; *dawcock, dawcake, and dawhawk*. They were recorded in Devon, and mean 'a stupid, silly awkward person'. This snatch of conversation was recorded towards the end of the last century: 'Polly Blackmore 'ath a-broked my best chinee taypot.' 'You shudden a-let zichee dawcake hannel tha tay thengs at all.'

Mrs M. Connolly of Waterford has been reading Mr T. Hardy of Dorset, and she wants to know what a *furner* is. It's a baker. Cotgrove in his 17th-century dictionary has '*fournier*, one that keeps or governs a common oven'.

'You won't believe this', writes a lady from Dunleer, 'but we country girls were often warned by our mothers about the *gancanagh*, a little fairy man, when we were young—and by young I mean in our teens. What does *gancanagh* mean?'

It means a man with an upturned nose (Irish *geancachán*); and your mothers were right to warn you, because he had the name of being a right boyo. 'A kind of fairy said to appear in lonesome valleys, making love to milkmaids', says the English Dialect Dictionary, adding, ambiguously, 'extremely common, especially near Drogheda'.

Beyond the Pale, and Some Celtic Words

Sheila Bradshaw of Strand Road in Sandymount wonders whether our (historical) Irish Pale gave rise to the expression *beyond the pale*—outside the limits of social convention.

No. *Pale* was the word used in common speech for any enclosure, from the 13th century down to the middle of the last one. 'I brought all my goods into this pale,' wrote Daniel Defoe, a man who also used the word in its primary meaning, a long board, pointed at the top and used for fences. He glossed the word *picket* as 'stakes stuck into one another like pales.'

As to Sheila's 'beyond the pale', I don't know when it was first seen in print; but Thomas Jefferson refers to 'the exercise of foreign jurisdiction within the pale of their own laws'. *Pale* is from Old French *pal*, a learned borrowing from Latin *palus*, a stake. It slipped into Irish as *páil*, and Dinneen has 'do ghreadhadh mar eachaibh i ngleacaíocht páil'—which he translates as 'who used to skim the fence like horses racing'. *Páil* also meant a stake or bar on which to hang a gate.

Miss E.P., who goes to school in Waterford, and who is too shy to let me print her name, wants to know whether Irish and the other Celtic languages had much of an influence on Old English.

The influence of Irish was small. In 563 Colm Cille came to Iona and stayed there for the remaining 34 years of his life. From Iona his missionaries went out to found other religious houses, and as a result of their work the words *anco* (hermit), *dry* (magician), *cross*, *clugge* (bell), *mind* (diadem), and *staer* (history) came into use in Old English. The Anglo-Saxons also picked up a few words from the Celtic languages through everyday contact with their neighbours; so we find *binn* (basket, crib), *bratt* (cloak), *brocc* (badger), *crag, luh* (lake), *cumb* (valley), *cine* (a gathering of parchment leaves), *torr* (projecting rock, peak), *dun* (dark-coloured). But when all is said and done, the Anglo-Saxons found little occasion to borrow words from the Celts, who were by then a submerged people. The Celtic influence in Britain remains, though, in the many placenames that have Celtic origins. But that's another story.

Arseward, Ballyragged, Amplush

A solicitor friend of mine tells me that in a case heard in a Waterford court a year or so ago, a man claimed to have been assaulted by a neighbour, and sent 'arseward backwards'. My friend asks if *arseward* is confined to the travelling community.

Arseward is as old as the 14th century, if not older. In parts of Wexford a horse is said to come arseward when it backs, and in Antrim the word can mean perverse, or obstinate. A Border poet called Stuart gave this advice back in 1686: 'Sae take some pity on your love/and do not still so arseward prove.' I like, too, the story about the Methodist preacher in Workington who enlightened his hears with: 'As wad a soon expect a swine to gang arsewurts up a tree and whissle like a throssie, as a rich man git to heaven.' *Arse* is from Old English, *ears*. Chaucer has the form *ers*. A taboo word, Collins calls it. Really?

'I'll not be *ballyragged*,' said a character in Carleton's story, *Fardorougha the Miser*. Mary Cantwell from Cork wants to know more about the word, which means to abuse violently, to scold or revile in foul language.

The great dictionaries say that it dates from the 18th century and that its origin is uncertain. It is probably a variant of *bullyrag* and it may very well have its origin in Oxford University slang. To bullyrag meant to turn a man's rooms upside down, to make 'hay' of them; and at the same place a ballyrag was the conclusion of a big student rag, a melée of gigantic proportions, by all accounts. The word is now more commonly used here in Ireland than across the water, I gather.

From a Mayo teacher comes a query about a word still used in Connacht, *amplush*. Carleton has this word; and so has Lover, and from the west. It is used as both a noun and a verb. As a noun it means a state of unreadiness, a disadvantage. 'There was no sitch thing as getting him at an amplush', wrote Lover. As a verb it meant to confuse in argument. Lover again: 'He'd have amplushed me long ago'. Simmons *Glossary of South Donegal English* says that the word was common also in Munster.

I have read that amplush is from the Irish *aimpléis*, glossed by O Dónaill as trouble, complication. The trouble is that *amplush* is found across the water from Scotland to Pembrokeshire. Both *aimpléis* and *amplush* arc corruptions of *non-plus*.

Forlorn Hope

Mathúin Mac Fheorais of Clonard Lawn, Dundrum, in Dublin, sent me an interesting and valuable gloss on *ladús/ladoose*, described by Ó Dónaill's dictionary as 'pert talk, sauciness; wheedling talk, cajolery; silly talk, non-sense', and by me, courtesy of a west Cork uncle, as mildly erotic, flirtatious talk. My correspondent tells me that both the noun and the adjectival form *ladúsach*, were used by his mother in Kilmurray MacMahon, Co. Clare.

Ladúsach to a Clare person means comfortable, cosy, well-off Mr Mac Fheorais has heard a woman say to a child in a cradle: 'Isn't it you are fine and ladúsach in there.' A well-to-do farmer would also be described as *ladúsach*. Brian Merriman has *ladús* in his masterpiece, and the late David Greene glossed it as 'ráiméis', nonsense, taking his cue from the Cork usage. My correspondent insists that the noun in Merriman's phrase describing the fast lady, 'Lán de ladús', would have, in Clare Irish, as it still does in Clare English, meant something like 'self-importance'. I have been told since the arrival of Mr Mac Fheorais's letter that both noun and adjective are still common in the rich English of his county.

Forlorn is a splendid word, and Mrs J. Barry, of Sutton, says that the headland, Forlorn Point, near Kilmore Quay, a place she describes as 'your old stomping ground', is well named, being desolate, deserted, forsaken. Ah, but Forlorn here is a corruption of the dialect *fur loan*, far land, and it has nothing to do with the standard word, which comes from Old English *forlorn*, lost. Which reminds me that the expression *forlorn hope* has nothing at all to do with hope. The folk (and false) etymology traces the expression to the Old English, but it from the Dutch *verloren hoop*, which literally means lost troop, the first soldiers or sailors to be sent into battle. They were not expected to survive. The French had their own name for them, *enfants perdus*, lost children. It seems that in the late 16th century the English sailors corrupted the Dutch expression, and called the doomed sailors *flowing hope*. It wasn't long before they etymologists 'corrected' this to *forlorn hope*.

Mr Martin Doyle of Cricklewood wants to know what the origin of *boss*, a straw cushion, is. It was used around Borris, Co. Carlow, in his youth. Swift had it in *Gulliver* (1727): 'Round which they sat on their haunches upon bosses of straw.' Apparently it is found nowadays only in parts of the south-east. It's related to the English dialect, *bass*, a hassock. Of unknown origin, I'm sorry to say.

Swail and Shucks!

Mrs A.S. from Raheny tells me that she is shy and English, and wonders what the origin of the word *swail*, which means shade, is. It was common in the Norfolk of her youth. She has never heard the word here in Ireland, where she has lived for the past thirty years.

The English Dialect Dictionary has this one, but under *swale*. John Clare once mused about being 'left in the swale and little cheered by sun'; and the English Dialect Dictionary gives an example from Norfolk, from Marshall's *Rural Economy* of 1787: 'Let us walk, or sit, in the swale.'

As far as I know the word has not been recorded in Ireland. It is of Norse origin. There is the Old Norse verb *svala*, to chill or cool; and the Icelandic *sval* a cool breeze.

Miss May Broderick of Limerick would like to know what the origin of the harmless American expletive *shucks!* is. She owns two good dictionaries, but they shelter behind the old reliable 'of uncertain origin', she says; so she wants me to go where Collins and Oxford fear to tread.

To be fair to the great dictionaries, most of them seem to think that it is related to *shuck*, a husk, pod, or shell. It came to mean a valueless thing: hence the interjection. The great Partridge, a man who knew the value of dialect guessed that shuck 'came from some Algonquin Indian word', and asked us to compare the Narragansett *anashuck*, shells. But as Miss Broderick has asked me to put my own head on the block, I now do so.

The word *shuck*, a spectre, has been used in English dialects since Chaucer was a garsún. This *shuck* was usually seen in the form of a dog. A hunt through the folklore of ghosts led me to this, reported in 1880: 'There is a notion prevalent in many places that whenever a calamity is at hand, or in localities where some accident or evil deed may have occurred, a spectral dog appears . . . this apparition is known under the name of *shuck*.'

This *shuck* is from Old English *scucca*, a demon. So is *shucks!* an English import, mild enough not to have upset the Puritan mores of a young America?

I'll tell you what leads me to believe that I may be right in my speculation, Miss B. It was something said by a Yorkshireman in a Wicklow hostelry recently, as we watched Mr Collins deposit Mr Eubank on his búndún. 'By all the shucks o' hell', he exclaimed. I rest my case.

Vareen, Dunt, Camalough

'Riding around the vareens mustn't be much fun,' said a Wexford horseman to me more than 25 years ago. He was talking about drag-hunting, a pursuit he thoroughly disapproved of. A *vareen* in SE Wexford is a headland.

Mrs June Leigh from Canterbury, tells me that she knows Co. Wexford well. She saw the word *vareen* in an edition of Poole's Glossary. Mrs Leigh wrote to question my etymology. Vareen, I confidently wrote, is from Irish *fearann*, land, territory. It can be found in glosses that are over a thousand years old. My correspondent argues that as *vareen* is not found outside the Barony of Forth, I should consider—given the origins of the dialect once spoken there—the West country dialect word *farren* as the real origin of the word.

Point taken, Mrs Leigh, I see that *farren* is, or was, a division of land, about an acre in Surrey and a half-acre in the West Country. This *farren* may be related to the *farundel* of land, a quarter of an acre, mentioned in Phillip's glossary of 1706.

But I'm still nor sure. Could *farren* have come from the older Irish *fearann*? Could they have a common ancestor? My trouble with both words is that neither really approximates to a headland. The Barony of Forth keeps her secret.

Mr J. Corboy of Limerick wants to know if *dunt*, a thump, is Irish. It is certainly very common here, but it is just as common in Scotland; and to judge from the frequency with which it was used in that country's literature, the Scots may rightly claim it. 'I'll tak dunts frae naebody,' wrote Burns, in a grumpy mood. Ballantine, in the last century, lamented that 'auld streets an' closes, wynds and houses, Wi sacrilegious dunts an' bruises are fa'ing fast'. Of the heart, *dunt* is to throb, palpitate. Burns, in a better mood, wrote: 'And while my heart wi' life-blood dunted, I'll bear't in mind.' The earliest dunt on record appeared in Douglas's *Eneados* in 1513: 'Nor as cowartis to eshew the first dunt.'

Finally, Mr Patrick Barry of Cork tells me that his father frequently used the word *camalough* when speaking of an ill-mannered person, a person who doesn't know his place. This is Irish *ceamalach*, a good Munster word. Why does Mr Will Carling come to mind.

Stour, Greip

Canon Noel Jackson of Moira, Craigavon, writes to enquire about a word frequently used in his part of the world by old people. The word is *stour*, a cloud of dust, and Canon Jackson says that he recently heard it from the lips of an eighty-year-old man when speaking about a dusty scullery. Many of the people who used the word have worked at some stage in textile mills.

Stour was certainly the word used for the dust that flies about flour mills. It seems not to have travelled south. Its southern counterpart was *dannock*

(Irish *deannach*, dust). The English Dialect Dictionary describes *stour* as dust in motion; used also of fine driven snow or chaff, or any substance in a state of powder.

The word is found all over Scotland and England and a turn-of-the-century Antrim man referred to the *stour* kicked up by the dancers in a barn. From *stour* we also have the adjective *stoury*, dusty: of the weather, characterised by driving clouds of dust or snow.

Stoor can also mean a quarrel, strife; bustle and confusion. Hence we have the Donegal *stooray*, a bold strap of a girl and the Scots *stoorie-woorie*, restless, excitable. 'Tween stoorie-woorie wife an' weans, Wow! but I'm cornered fairly', wrote a minor Lanackshire poet a century ago.

Stour came from the Anglo-French *estur*, from Old French *estour*, *estorn*, conflict, tumult. These words, however, are Germanic in origin. Compare Old High German *sturm* and modern German *sturm*, storm.

Charles Acton asks about the northern word for a dung-fork, *greip*, the counterpart of our southern *sprong*. It is of Scandinavian origin. The Norwegian dialect word is *greip*, the Danish *greb*. *Sprong* is an English dialect word, related to *prong*, and it has been assimilated into Irish. Why not? It's a good word.

Tugging the Katshee and Other Matters

'Talk of plámás! She tugs the katshee to everybody that one.' Thus spake the granny of Mrs Breeda Smith, late of Co. Monaghan, now living in Dublin. Mrs Smith has sent me a list of her granny's words and phrases and asks for help with some of them. First of all, *pulling the katshee*. *Katshee* is a corruption of the Irish *céad dlaoi*, the forelock. *Céad* is first, foremost; *dlaoi* is lock, tress.

The next word is *drawky*, an adjective used by honest northerners to describe the miserable, wet, drizzly, depressing weather the rest of us call 'soft'. The English Dialect Dictionary has traced drawky to Ireland, Scotland and the northern counties of England. There is also the verb *drawk*, meaning to soak, drench; and the Scots poet, William Dunbar, in 1510 used *drawkit* in one of his less earthy efforts . . . 'his pennis war drowned and drawkit.' *Pennis* means feathers, by the way. Well where did it come from, this old word? The English Dialect Dictionary refuses to hazard a guess, which surprises me. I'm pretty sure it's related to Old Norse *drukna*, wet, which would make it a relative of the Ulster *drookit*.

Yorks (always plural) is an interesting word. They are the bands of twisted straw or hay that farmers and farm-workers in the old days used to tie around their trousers below the knee; a kind of garter to keep the trouser ends up and free of muck and clabber. The word is to be found in various little glossaries of Irish English. No trace of *yorks* in the English Dialect Dictionary or in the standard dictionaries. Could it be that it is a corruption of the Irish word *iarach*, a binding?

Finally, Gerard Condra, a Limerickman based in Munich, and P. O'Beirne from London, wrote to me about the Munster word *bowjanter*, variously a creamery churn, a large bottle of stout, a funnel for straining creamery milk. Mr C. suggests *pot de chambre* (I don't think so somehow); and Mr O'Beirne suggests *pot champêtre*. The latter may be right. If he is, my friend Alan Harrison, who also suggested it, gets a lick of the lollipop.

Slink, Grush and Gruff

Mrs Mary Fahy, who tells me she would have been a neighbour of the poet Raftery had they been contemporaries, wants to know if the noun *slink*, a contemptible *sleeveen*, and the adjective *slinky*, cunning, deceitful, come from Irish.

They don't, although they appear often in Anglo-Irish literature. 'He's blackguardin' and blastin' away at that quare slink-lookin chap upstairs,' wrote Lover in *Handy Andy* (1842). You'll find *slink*, all over the neighbouring island and in America too.

There is a related, rare word, found by Prof. Tomás de Bhaldraithe in an early *c.*19th manuscript, and heard by him in Ballyglunin, Co. Galway, not far from Mary Fahy's birthplace. This is *slincín*, a still-born animal or child. Prof. de Bhaldraithe identifies this word as the English dialect word *slink*. (Never mind the *-ín*; we have a habit of Gaelicising English words by adding the diminutive suffix.)

The English Dialect Dictionary had this *slink* as a noun and verb common in Scotland, England and America; there is no mention of Ireland. *Slink* can also mean the flesh of a prematurely born calf; inferior or diseased meat. 'Three cows slinked, the mare followed suit', was recorded in America. In England we find *slinker* a cow which casts its calf. *Slink*, in all its forms, comes from Old English *slincan*.

Donal Cummins of Glenbeigh Park, Dublin 7, wants to know the origin of *grush*, the scramble for small change thrown to children in some parts of Dublin after a wedding. In his father's day it was common to heat the coins on a shovel before throwing them, he tells me. *Grush* is related to the English dialect verb *grush*, to crumble; to the Scots *gruss*, to press, crush or squeeze. It is a word of Germanic origin, related to the East Frisian *grusen*.

Another g-word, *groof*. I wonder has my valued correspondent, Robert Sharpe from Glenariffe, Co. Antrim, this one? I heard it from a Ballymena visitor to a Wicklow rugby pub recently. He was complimenting Mr Eric Cantona on giving that gentleman who annoyed him a beauty straight in the *groof*. *Groof*, sometimes spelled *gruff*, *grouf* and *grufe*, is a good Scots word for the belly. Selkirkshire's Christopher North (fl. 1820) in his *Noctes Ambrosianae*, used may good Scots words still heard in the north of Ireland, including *gruff*: 'Creeping stealthily on my gruff, I laid mysel' a' my length alang hers.'

That's as far as he got, if you're interested.

Smoor, Smurdikeld and Smoorich

The estimable Father Dinneen has the word *smúr* for a slight shower of rain, and so has a lady who writes from Kingscourt, Co. Cavan. Dinneen defines smúr as 'embers, cinders, dross, mist, vapour, a cloud of dust, a shower, grime.' He seems to be in two minds as to whether the word is Irish at all, and tells us to compare the Irish *múr*, a shower, and the English *smoor*. I think he was wrong about *smoor* if he had 'shower' in mind.

They have the word in Wexford as a verb, in the forms *to smore*, and *to smoor*, to suffocate. The English Dialect Dictionary recorded it mainly in Scotland and in the north of England. 'By this time he was cross the ford,/Whare in the snaw the chapman smoor'd', wrote Burns in *Tam O'Shanter*. 'Smoor the light', 90-year-old Phil Wall from Carne said to me once as we left his house to go for a pint. 'Smure the candle' was recorded in Aberdeen.

In Yorkshire they have a lovely word that is derived from smoor—*smurdikeld*, which comes from the phrase *smoor'd in the keld*. The English Dialect Dictionary explains: 'when a foal comes to the birth without assistance, having a kell or caul over its nostrils, and there being no one near to remove it, the animal dies for want of air to the lungs.' This smoor/smore comes from the Old English *smorian*, to choke, suffocate; for this reason we needn't be surprised to find it in the Barony of Forth, where, until the beginning of the 19th century they spoke a dialect of English in which Chaucer would have felt at home.

The word *smúrach* gave me a lot of trouble recently. I heard it in the Rosses of Donegal years ago, and I was told it meant a sloppy kiss. Dinneen was of no help: Smúrach: 'black dust, dry soot, smouldering ashes,' I dismissed his Smúrdáil: 'sniffing, smelling around, half-hearted rooting, dozing'; and his Smúrthacht: 'sniffing as a dog on the track of game, or a cow over bad fodder.'

I think I have found the answer under *Smoorich* in the English Dialect Dictionary (*Ich* pronounced as the German *Ich*). A Scottish word, which won't surprise you. It means a kiss, and it has many variants, including *smurick* and *smurach*. 'She ever and anon took some refreshment in the shape of an occasional smoorich, which fully accounted for the cheepin' I heard', said a Forfarshire eavesdropper. Is it related to the OE *smorian*, to suffocate, I wonder? I must find a Rosses woman and ask her if it fits the bill.

Anathema

Isn't it strange how words have, in the course of the centuries, come to mean their opposite. *Anathema* is one of these. The Greek word, *anatithenai*, from *ana*, up + *tithenai*, to set, was applied to something set aside as an offering to a god. It was devoted to the god; but since such things were usually sacrificed, the word came to mean doomed, accursed. It subsequently came to mean a detested person or thing, a formal ecclesiastical curse, or a formal denuncia-tion of a doctrine. Recently I noted that the word was often used by political commentators speculating on the relationship between two parties now in government together. Because these parties were held to be anathema to one another, the situation was considered to be a *farce* by one commentator.

Farce is another word that has changed its meaning considerably. As far back as the 14th century it meant stuffing, and one stuffed fowl with *farcemeat*, chopped up herbs and spices. It came into English through Old French from the Latin verb *farcire*, to stuff, which to the ecclesiastical gentlemen of yore meant to interpolate passages in church services, religious plays etc. This ecclesiastical stuffing, about as subtle as a sheep's head, came to be called *farce*. Then farce came to mean, in secular theatre, the funny interludes stuffed between the acts of a serious drama, by the likes of Cervantes and Lope de Vega in Spain, and by the Tudors in their post-play *gigs* and *jigs*.

Bombast is another word that I heard applied to the Dáil interpolations of one whose duty it is to interpolate. Another word, this, that has changed its meaning. Nowadays it means pompous and grandiloquent language; but to the Norman ladies in their dank castles *bombax* was simply the cotton stuff they padded cushions and pillows with, while their lordships were out putting manners on the Irish. So *bombast* comes from *bombax*, and it in turn comes from the Medieval Latin, *bombax*, cotton.

Speaking of the Normans, Ann Murphy from Kildare asks about the word *motty*, the stone at which the pennies were thrown to determine who would toss first in pitch-and-toss. This is the French *motte*, the butt at which arrows were shot when knights were bold. Pitch-and-toss is an ancient game, and let me tell you, Ann, that none of your Kildare tossers could hold a candle to Abdul Malik (fl. 700 AD). This sporting gentleman is credited with having tossed heads seven times in a row—to win Syria.

Some Handlin'

The influence of Scotland has crossed the waters of the Moyle into Ulster, in language as in other matters. But the late John Braidwood sounded a warning note when he wrote of 'the pusillanimous notions of correctness and good taste hammered into kids in school, deterring their progress along the highway of their native tongue, the byeways being prohibited'. My friend Benedict Kiely has also written about the equally malign influence of radio and television, and there are many who believe that the dialect that owes its richness to Scots is very much endangered.

I was touched recently to receive a copy of a delightful little book called *Some Handlin'* from a reader, Mr David Hogg, who lives in Sion Mills, near Strabane. It is a collection of words and phrases gathered by the pupils of Ballyrashane Primary School, near Coleraine, in 1986, under the direction of an inspired teacher, Mrs Rae McIntyre. In the second edition (1990) Mrs McIntyre proudly stated that 'since the first edition of the book was compiled there has been a perceptible change in attitude towards non-standard dialect . . . it is now regarded as a distinctive aspect of our cultural heritage.'

What a wonderful little book it is! With its Scots base, and a wee sprinkling of Irish and its funny illustrations drawn by the children, it should interest people who live far from Coleraine.

How many of these words would Rab Burns have known?— *Black neb*: a Presbyterian (*neb*, a face). *Birces*: anger. 'Tanya's birces would get up very quickly.' *Brattle*: the noise of thunder. *Broo*: edge (Irish *bruach*). 'He cleaned out the sheugh an' put all the glar on the broo.' *Clart*: a very untidy girl. *Clemmed*: cold and wet. *Clift*: a very silly woman. *Claits*: *feet. Clouter*: a cough. *Coom*: turf-mould (ME *culme*, coal dust). *Corbie*: a crow (French *corbin*). *Dashlin*: second-best clothes. *Drookit*: wet (Old Norse *drukna*). *Frae me-come-tae-me*: a trombone. *Glar*: mud, drookit stoor (Irish, *glár*). *Loanin*: a lane. *Nyuk*: to steal. 'He would nyuk the hole out of a flute.' *Oory*: unwell looking. *Sevendible*: severe.

This wonderful little book (80 pp) was published by North-West Books, Main Street, Limavady, at £3.95. Perhaps it's still in print.

A sad note. In her introduction Mrs McIntyre wrote: 'Unfortunately a falling enrolment means that Ballyrashane Primary School will close within the next few years. Hopefully the success of this effort means that we will end with a bang rather than a whimper.'

That you've done, Mrs McIntyre. That you've done.

Overright, Minikin, Paddle and Pill

Mr J. O'Sullivan from Killarney asks where we got the word *overright*, meaning in front of, opposite. He came across the word in Griffin's *The Collegians*. It came to being from a confusion regarding the Irish word *comhair*, used only in the prepositional phrase, *os comhair*, and meaning opposite, and the noun *cóir*, right, equity. *Os* is over; somewhere along the way, somebody, perhaps a hedge schoolmaster, confused *comhair* and *cóir*, which are pronounced identically; and thus we got *overright*, instead of something like 'over opposite'.

Mrs Jenny Weir, who was born near Coleraine, asks if we have the lovely word *minikin* in the south. I heard *minikeen* from the late Mrs Elizabeth Jeffries of Kilmore, Co Wexford, a quarter of a century ago. To Mrs Weir *minikin* is an adjective, meaning little, neat: 'the wee minikin bairn'. To Mrs Jeffries it was a noun, used only of a girl who was small and sexy; a pocket Venus who was aware of her charms. *Minikin is* found in Scotland, and no doubt it found its way to Coleraine from there; it is also found in England's West Country, which may account for its presence in the barony of Bargy. It is an old word, and it was used to effect by your man from Warwickshire. 'For one blast of thy minikin mouth/Thy sheep shall take no harm,' he wrote in *Lear*.

Another old word from the north, this time from Miss Anne McMullan from Belfast, who heard it near Cushendall. A waitress said to a man who was getting increasingly annoyed by a small child of his who was intent on wrecking a hotel diningroom: 'Ach don't say a word to him. He's only lookin' for attention. Paddle the wee scaldie.' It turned out, that the Antrim woman's *paddle* was an old verb that meant, to handle or feel lovingly. It is now found only in the north of Ireland, in Scotland and in Devon, according to a recent survey. But our friend Shakespeare had it. Do you remember your *Othello?*—'Didst thou not see her paddle with the Palm of his hand?' The word is thought to be related to *pad* to move softly, furtively, from Middle Dutch *paden*, Collins speculates.

Finally, a query from an old friend who lives in my home town of New Ross. What, he wants to know, is the origin of *pill*, a creek, a bye-water of a tidal river? He reminds me that we both learned to swim in a particularly dangerous one near Roche's of Ballyanne. Pill is from Old English *pyll*, pool.

County Dublin Invective

A lady who lives in Newcastle, Co. Dublin, writes to tell me that some of her elderly friends have a line in invective that would put some of our Dáil deputies to shame; and she wonders where in God's name did the following words originate. The first is *quilt*. No, not the substitute for a blanket, but a mischievous, conniving person.

Quilt is not in Joseph Wright's monumental English Dialect Dictionary; the cant and slang dictionaries don't have it either. I'm pretty sure that it is a corruption of the Irish *cuileat*, the knave in card games, extended to describe human and animal villains. Dinneen has *cuileat capaill*, a vicious horse. I've heard the word *quilt* in Dublin city and in the neighbouring counties, and I wonder how widespread it is.

My correspondent's second word she spells *rawsie*. This is another word that has escaped the nets of Wright, Partridge, and the rest. A *rawsie*, I am told, is 'a strap of a girl'. She would be known in Dublin town as a *rozzie*. I have no doubt about this word either. It's the Irish word *rásaí*, a variant of *rásach*, defined by Dinneen as 'a rambling woman, a gypsy, a jilt'.

Another type of girl not in favour with the matriarchs of south Co. Dublin is the *clip*. A clip, mind you, wouldn't be gone as far down the road to perdition as a *rawsie*; my friend describes her as 'a brazen hussy'. The English Dialect Dictionary has *clip*, from both Ireland and Scotland. It originally meant a foal; then it came to mean a mischievous, naughty girl. The English Dialect Dictionary has 'a'll gie it tae ye for that, ye clip', from the *Ballymena Observer* (1892). I have little doubt that clip is from Irish *cliobóg*, a colt, a filly; the Antrim variety by way of Scottish Gaelic. Why, you might ask, is clip confined to a frisky young female? I don't know.

My correspondent's last word is especially interesting. It is a compound noun which she spells *mogalleenmire*. She writes: 'I've heard women counselling girls going out with young men they heartily approved of saying, "Be sure now to give him the mogaleen mire".' Easy now, gentle reader; the *mogaleen mire* is the Irish *magairlín meidhreach*, the early purple orchid, *Orchis mascula*, used for centuries to make a love potion. As for the literal meaning of the two Irish words, I'm afraid I'm altogether too demure to tell you. I must refer you to Father Dinneen. Suffice to say that methinks the plant was most aptly named.

Giglet and Strone

A word I had forgotten was sent to me recently by a friend of the late Mrs Liz Jeffries of Kilmore in Co. Wexford. The word is *giglet* and in that part of the world it meant a lighthearted girl, a bit of a tomboy. In Scotland the word is common still, and I'm told it is to be found, too, in many parts of southern England.

It is an old word. Shakespeare has it in Henry VI: 'Young Talbot was not born to be the pillage of a giglet wench'; but here the word is used to signify a wanton, a strumpet.

Giglet is, I fancy, related to giggling, a word also found in the forms *gigleting* and *giggleting*. 'Who's more vor giggleting than thee art thysel?', asked a Devon girl 200 years ago, in a dialect that shared many characteristics with the English spoken in Kilmore at that time. Mrs Jeffries had *gigleting*.

The English Dialect Dictionary tells us that in Dorset from time immemorial young girls have been in the habit on Lady Day of standing in the market-places awaiting the chance of being hired as servants. The fair was known as Giglet Fair. In the parish of Our Lady's Island, in Wexford's Barony of Forth, the Lady Day fair was known as Illone Vaar (Island Fair). *Giglet* is related to French argot *gigolette,* glossed by Delasalle as 'grisette, faubourienne courant les bals publics.'

The interesting word *strone* was sent to me by a lady from Antrim town who wants to remain anonymous. 'I well remember,' she says, 'that in my very first day at school over sixty years ago now, the teacher was quite amazed because I said "I want to go out to strone!" To *strone* meant to pee, and we used the word all the time at home.'

A good Scots word this. Burns writing about a dog in 1786 has 'an' stroan't on stanes an' hillocks wi' him.' There is an old Scots belief that on Halloween the deil stroans on the haws—the pooka's misdemeanour here in Ireland.

Stroan is also a noun meaning a stream, a runlet of water; and it is found all over Northern England and Scotland. In Donegal it means the stream of milk got from a cow at one pull. The major dictionaries say that the word is of unknown origin. Surely to God it is the Scots Gaelic—and Irish—*sruthan,* a stream, in disguise?

Polthogue, Sorra and Smit

James Reilly, a Co. Cavan man with an address in Dover, writes to ask where the word *polthogue* comes from. His mother, he tells me, used it frequently when young Master Reilly was up to no good. It means a clout, a blow, and is used in most Irish counties.

The word is the Irish *paltóg,* but where did this word come from? I think it may have come from English, and a long time ago too. Consider the evidence. The word *polt,* and its variants *poult, powlt* and *pult* are found in English dialects from Northumberland to the Isle of Wight. As a verb it means to beat, strike, and according to the English Dialect Dictionary, to knock down fruit from trees with a long pole. Hence they have *poulting iron,* an instrument used in the old days for beating the awns off barley; and William Cobbett, writing from Hampshire, told his farm manager to give a bone-idle blackguard he had given a job to 'a good pulting with a strong stick'. The oldest form in English is to be found in a manuscript dated 1225: 'Hit wule poulten on him.'

A Letterkenny reader asks about the origin of the word *sorra* often used in 19th-century Irish novels, but seldom heard nowadays. She remembers her grandmother using such sentences as 'sorra the bit did he ever do for us'. *Sorra* is *sorrow* (Old English and Old Norse *sorg*) and it has been used since medieval times both as a euphemism for the Devil and as an emphatic negative.

These secondary usages of sorrow/sorra/sarra survive only in Scotland and Ireland as far as I know. 'She doesn't give herself many airs but her people were as proud as the very sarra,' wrote Carleton in *Fardorougha the Miser* (1848). Seumus MacManus of Donegal wrote about 'a black treacherous bog in a night as sleety and as wet as sorra'. Fergusson, in his interesting travel book *Rambles* (1884) says that in Orkney 'devil is called Sorrow'. I wonder how common *sorra* still is.

I heard an interesting word from a northern punter at the Leopardstown Christmas meeting. Rumour had it that Danoli had coughed. 'Surely to God Tom Foley won't run him when he has the smit,' said my friend. Tom Foley, sadly, did. The *smit* (always singular) means an infection. *Smit* is a very old word, confined nowadays to northern England, Scotland and the north of Ireland. It comes from Old English *smitta*, a spot.

Rocket, Kitchen, Lambaste

Mrs Ann Ryan, a Limerick woman, tells me that many years ago, her husband was not a little troubled on hearing Granny who had come to stay for Christmas, announce that she had purchased a *rocket* as a present for her grandaughter, aged six. The rocket turned out to be a dress, and Mrs Ryan tells me that the word was common in rural Limerick in her youth.

The English Dialect Dictionary has it, too, and from Antrim. In Scotland it is described as 'a loose upper cloak'; and there is a reference to a man who appeared at his trial in 1812 dressed 'in a very rich suit . . . and a scarlet rocket'. But where did the word come from? From France: it is the Norman French *rochet*, or *roquet*, a frock.

Another interesting word came from an Omagh reader. The word is *kitchen*, and it doesn't mean the place where a cook works. No, this kitchen means anything eaten as a relish with bread, potatoes, or other plain fare. 'Butter to butter's no kitchen', was an Ulster saying, and the English Dialect Dictionary gives 'We have no kitchen to our praties, not even a bit of cabbage', as coming from Cavan. 'Hunger is a good kitchen,' wrote Kelly in a book called *Proverbs*, back in 1721—a saying Irish speakers would recognise as 'Is maith an t-anlann an t-ocras.'

To kitchen was a verb in common use all over Ireland in the last century. 'Instead of drinking his little earnings in a sheebeen house, and then eating his praties dry, he'd take care to have something to kitchen them,' wrote Carleton; and Patrick Kennedy from Wexford complained that they were 'without a single piece of meat to kitchen our potatoes'. Is *kitchen* still in use in this sense?

James Hegarty from Cork wants to know where the word *lambaste*, meaning to thrash, comes from. It is found only in Ireland and in Lincoln-shire, according to the English Dialect Dictionary. 'Glad I wasn't standing in his shoes when the mistress was lambasting him,' wrote the P. Kennedy

mentioned above. *Lambaste* comes from a combination of two old Scandinavian words, both of which mean to beat mercilessly: Old Norse *lemja*, and
Old Icelandic *beysta*. *To lam*, meaning to thrash, and *lamming,* a thrashing,
are still common in Ireand; and as for *baste*, I'll leave the last word to Samuel
Pepys about the love of his life. 'I took a broom and basted her till she cried
extremely,' he confided to his diary on 1 December 1660.

Garble, Astonish

That good old verb *to garble* is, in the sense 'to separate the good from the
bad' now obsolete, according to an article in a learned journal I read recently.
It is no such thing: it is alive and well in parts of counties Carlow, Wexford,
Waterford and Tipperary, I am reliably informed. Greyhound pups are let
out in the yard to be garbled by prospective buyers; bins of spices were
garbled in Chaucer's time.

Garble in this sense has a long and interesting history. It came from Low
Latin, *garba*, a sheaf of wheat, from Old Italian *garbellare*, to sift. This word is
from the Arabic *gharballa*, to sift, from *ghirbal*, a sieve; the Arabs, however,
had borrowed it from the Latin, *cribrum*, a sieve. The Restoration writer,
Fuller, would be pleased to know that *garble*, as he used the verb, is still alive
somewhere. In a panegyric on King Charles he wrote: 'Garbling men's
manners you did well divide, To take the Spaniards' wisdom, not their pride.'
And in an account of London, he tells us that 'there was a fair hospital built
to the honour of St Anthony the protectors and proctors whereof claimed
the privilege to themselves to garble the live pigs in the markets of the city,
and such as they found starved or unwholesome they would slit in the ear,
tie a bell about their necks and turn them loose about the city.' Returning
them to the care of the community, as they say in Hawkins Street.

In parts of Maryland and Pennsylvania, *to astonish* hasn't yet completely
loosened itself from its etymology, as it has done everywhere else. (Old
French *estoner,* from Vulgar Latin *extonare,* to strike with thunder). Nowadays
an astonished person can hardly be said to be struck by thunder; but to the
descendants of the early English settlers in America to be astonished means
to be suddenly and violently struck. Milton would understand. 'In matters
of religion, blind astonished and struck with superstition as with a planet,'
said he of monks. Nobody would have to interpret Holland, the translator
of Livy, for the Chesapeake Bay fishermen either, 'the knaves that lay in wait
behind rose up and rolled down two huge stones, whereof one smote the
king upon the head, the other astonished his shoulder.' In rural Maryland
some newspapers until recent times reported cases of assault and battery as
cases of astonishment.

My regards to Paul Strain, attorney-at-law, from Baltimore, whose grandfather came from the Rosses, Co. Donegal.

Wha' cheer, boy?

Eoin C. Bairéad, from Dublin's Harold's Cross, tells me of a greeting used in the town of Cobh in days gone by. Old timers whose paths hadn't crossed for a while would say *'Wha' cheer, boy?'*

This greeting, which, for all I know, may still be used in Cork, is as old as Tudor times. In *A Midsummer Night's Dream,* Theseus says to his beloved Queen of the Amazons, 'Come, my Hippolyta; what cheer, my love?' In Durham, according to a correspondent of Joseph Wright, the greatest of the dialect lexicographer. 'What cheer! is the commonest greeting of man to man, answered back in the same words.' The greeting has also been recorded in Yorkshire, 'What cheer, awd boy?' to an ordinary acquaintance; 'What cheer, my hearty?' to an intimate friend. I am told that the old greeting is also the basis for the Cockney *wocher/*and the Suffolk *Watchee!*

Mary Kelly from Galway, just back from a holiday in the USA, wants to know why our *sweets* are their *candy.* All I know is that the Tudor English for sweets was candy, and that the children of the emigrants to America kept the old word. Shakespeare used candy as an adjective—'What a candy deal of courtesy'—as well as a verb, meaning to sweeten. Both Shakespeare and Kit Marlowe used the now obsolete *discandy,* for melt away or dissolve.

Which reminds me that *treacle,* Old French *triacle* from Latin *theriaca,* antidote for a bite, began life in English as just that. Lydgate called the holy name, Jesus, the 'holsomest tryaicle'. Treacle used as a salve gave its name to the Treacle Bible. Milton wrote of 'the Sovran treacle of sound Doctrine', following the medieval usage of the word. Treacle has, you might say, come to a sticky end.

Skelp, Woar, Skip

Mr S.J. Kingston, who hails from Kent but who has been living in west Cork for many years, asks whether the word *skelp,* a slap, is Irish. He has never heard the word in England, but notes that it is recorded in the major dictionaries.

Mr Kingston is not the only Englishman to be intrigued by this word. Not very far from where he lives, another, fictional, Englishman pondered this question of origin near Lisheen, after the races. You may remember Slipper's conversation with Major Yates in the Somerville and Ross story:

'Skelp her, ye big brute, says I. What good's in ye that aren't able to skelp her?"
. . . Leigh Kelvey was sufficiently moved to ask me if skelp was a local term.'

Skelp is English, but has long been adopted by us Irish as *sceilp*.The word
is not recorded in the English Dialect Dictionary. It seems that it is rare
enough in rural England; a pity, this, because it is as old as the *York Mysteries*
of 1440, where we find 'He shal be with schath of skelpys yll scarred.' Burns
in *Contented Wi' Little* has 'I gie them a skelp as they're creepin' alang'. I'm
told that the word is rarely used in Scotland nowadays. I'm at a loss to explain
why *skelp* was ignored by the English Dialect Dictionary. Was it because it
was regarded as a standard word?

Richard Roche, the historian of Norman Wexford and of Wexford's
coast, asks what the origin of the word *woar* is. We both have used this word
for seaweed since childhood, and I had assumed it was standard English. It
is not. We find the word in print for the first time in Holinshed's *History of
Ireland* (1586) where 'the woar of the sea' is referred to. Nothing before that,
and nothing after. The English Dialect Dictionary hasn't got it. Oxford
speculates that its origin may be *ore,* an old word for kelp. Maybe. But why
not go back further to the Old English *war,* seaweed.

Miss M. Monroe (eh?), who says she is a Trinity student, wants to know
why the college servants are called *skips*. Apparently this word is short for
skip-kennel, a derisory term used by Swift for a lackey, or manservant. Oxford
guesses that originally the term meant one who had to jump over the kennels
or gutters; a mean sort of person.Why these persons spent their working
hours jumping kennels I can't quite figure out, but as for being mean, Miss
M. would agree that the description still fits the bill. She tells me that the
skips flung her out of the Trinity Ball last year, just because she happened to
be lingering under her boyfriend's bed without a ticket.The crathur!

Disguised and Gawky

Samuel Lover was fond of using the word *disguised*. He glossed it for his
readers, assuring them that it was widely used in the west of Ireland. A good
job, too; what would you make of this sentence without his footnote: 'You
don't know me bekos I'm disguised.' 'Here be a mummer, or a wren-boy,'
I said to myself, but I was wrong; Lover's footnote said: 'disguised means
drunk'.

The word also crops up in the South of England.The English Dialect
Dictionary has this from Kent: 'I'd rather not say he was exactly drunk, but
he seemed as though he was jes' a little bit disguised.' I wonder is the word
still in use anywhere in Ireland?

Mr Joe Hayes of Limerick, wrote to ask what the origin of the word *gawky*
is. A gawky hurler, he says, is one whose right hand is placed before his left

on the hurley; an *amalach* sort of player, says my correspondent. Amalach means awkward, and *gawke* is defined in Grose's great dictionary of 1790 as 'an awkward type'. It is cognate with the French *gauche*. It is a well-travelled word. Burns has 'Gawkies, Taupies, Gowks and Fools/Frae colleges an' boarding schools'; and Taylor, a lesser man, advised a friend in 1787: 'Go hame and woo some country gawkie.'

Speaking of hurling, the aforementioned Mr Lover used the expression *we have taken the ball at the hop* in *Handy Andy*. It came from hurling. Mr Hayes, I'm sure, will long remember that second great goal of Offaly's.

Jeanette Huber, of Scilly, Kinsale, an American lady with Irish antecedents, and now an Irish citizen, is intrigued by *dydee*, a worthless ornament. A *dydee* to her Irish relatives living in America is what we would call a baby's nappy; it was, she feels, a word brought from Ireland by her grandparents. I find this interesting, because another correspondent, Mary Kelly, of Dolphin's Barn, Dublin, tells me that she heard a lady of the old school giving out about a young wan of her acquaintance frolicking in Brittas Bay 'in nothing but the tiniest dydee of a knickers'.

All I can say is that *dydee*, from Clare to Derry means a trinket, and that the words *daighsín* and *daighdín* mean the same thing. I'm not sure where the *daigh* in the two Irish words comes from. *Daig* is explained as '*tug*, he gave', in O'Clery's Glossary; perhaps *dydee* is related somehow to 'a little present'. Which, of course, won't tie in with either Jeanette's diaper or Mary's knickers. I must investigate further.

Whisht!

From the bush, somewhere outside Mowze in Zambia, came a nice letter from Fr Conall Ó Cuinn, S.J. In the course of it he suggests that the interjection *whisht!*, be silent, may come from the Irish *tost*, silence, through some phrase such as *bi id thost*. I've heard this etymology before; but it's a false one, I'm afraid. *Whisht* has been around in English since the 14th century, as a verb, a noun, an interjection, an adjective, and an adverb. Both Surrey and Spenser have *to whist*, to silence; Scott has 'the deil's in ye; will ye whisht' in *Waverley*; and the English Dialect Dictionary's correspondents sent in the noun *whisht* to Oxford from Ireland, Scotland, the Isle of Man, Lincolnshire, Yorkshire, Norfolk, Kent and Suffolk. Even the 'Irish' "hould your whisht", is found all over Britain. 'You need na doubt I held my whisht', wrote Burns in *The Vision*, his one and only *aisling*. 'Hold yer whisht an lissen', was reported from Yorkshire.

A child from Wordsworth's lake country said that 'the owl flies very whisht'; another from Kent described herself 'a whisht child, usually'.

So where does it come from, this word we like to claim as our own? No one knows. I think, it is related to such words as *hist* and *hush*—a good dialect onamatopaeic word, as old as the English language, and maybe older.

J. Kenny wrote from Limerick asking about the *Fiddler's Green* mentioned in the song. It is the traditional heaven of sailors who die ashore, and according to Partridge it is a late 18th-century expression. F. Bowen's *Sea Slang* (1929) defines this Elysium as 'a place of unlimited rum and tobacco'. Marryat, in *Snarley Bow* has: 'A Fiddler's Green, where seamen true,/When here they've done their duty,/The bowl of grog shall still renew,/And pledge to love and beauty.'

Anne O'Reilly of Youghal asks about a Cork City expression. 'Have you ever heard the phrase *she gave me fifty*, meaning "she stood me up?" ' she asks. The expression is new to me, and the Cork friends I've asked are at a loss to explain its origin. One of them suggests a link with the English expression, 'to play with fifty', that is to play with a deck that is two cards short; in other words, not to play absolutely fair.

Finally, Mary Friel from Derry wants to know where the northerners' *till* in such sentences as 'I went till Portrush on my holidays' comes from. From our Scandinavian friends, by way of Scotland. From the Old Norse preposition, *til*, to.

Words from County Louth

Professor Etienne Rynne of UCG, the archaeologist, once took time off from his professional duties hokin' at Kilkerley, near Dundalk, to record many dialect words from local people, and he has kindly sent me a copy of this valuable collection published in the *Journal of the Co. Louth Archaeological and Historical Society* in 1980. Many of the words he wrote down are new to me, and I'm at a loss as to their origins. Considering that I failed recently to recognise the Westmeath word *trawlick* as Irish *trálach,* a word I've known since I was about five, I throw out some of Etienne Rynne's words to my readers, hoping that they may jolt my flagging memory into life.

Collyer: A pinkeen or minnow; also an old cow. (I've heard a former British PM, who shall be nameless, described as a *callaire,* but this Irish word, common enough now in the English of West Cork, is glossed by Dinneen as a female scold, not an old cow.) *Hasky:* cold, sharp and windy. 'That's a hasky day.' *Gawtherens:* men who travel around helping with the harvest. (*Gátar,* poverty, hunger, springs to mind; perhaps it shouldn't.) *Mararoogle,* also *Melloroodle:* the fruit of the burdock. *Stry:* A lazy, untidy woman. A form of *straoil,* anglicised street, a slovenly woman?

I'm not sure, because Rynne also has *Strying:* moving around from house to house, gossiping etc. *Tallyeh:* a stiffness of wrist. A form of my friend *trálach?*

Mary O'Connell from the city by the Lee wonders where we got the term *in the pink*? Is this, she wonders, an Americanism, and why *pink*?

The phrase is English in origin. Pink is a colour and pink is a flower; and the colour was named from the flower. The colour pink was not so named until the 18th century; the flower was named sometime in the 16th. Nobody is quite sure what the origin of pink is. Collins has traced it to *pinkeye,* a partial translation of obsolete Dutch *pinck oogen,* little eyes; this is sensible: consider that the French for the flower is *œillet* At any rate, this Old World plant of the genus *Dianthus,* was renowned for its fragrance. Phrases which reflect the highest or best degree or condition, such as the one mentioned by the lady from Cork, derive ultimately from the esteem in which the flower was held long ago. The pink was, to the great playwright who died tragically in Deptford, 'the flower of flowers'; and you may remember his even greater contemporary . . . *Mercutio*: Nay, I am the very pink of courtesy. *Romeo*: Pink for flower. *Mercutio*: Right.

The New Testament in Scots

One of my most treasured books is one I bought about ten years ago. Anthony Burgess had called it 'un libro muy importante' in *El País.* The poet, Peter Levi, said that it was marvellously alive. George Bruce called it a great prose work. Alan Bold said that it was majestic, and John Whale, to put the minds of pedants at rest, said that it was trenchant, vivid, and *faithful*. I am referring to the late W.L. Lorimer's *The New Testament in Scots* and if you don't already possess it, you might be lucky and find the Penguin paperback.

Lorimer spent most of his life teaching Greek in his native Scotland and I suppose it was inevitable that a man who had also taken up the study of the Scots language at the age of nine, should translate the New Testament. He never saw his great work in print. He was revising it when he died, but his well-taught son finished the job for him using his voluminous notes. He recreated Scots prose in this wonderful work, and for me, at least, he recreated the gospels. Young people who have read only the anaemic English version they now read in schools and churches should read this book. Here is a little from Matthew.

> Meantime Peter wis sittin furth i the close, when a servan-queyn cam up an said till him, 'Ye were wi the man frae Galilee, Jesus, tae, I'm thinkin.'
>
> But he denied it afore them aa: 'I kenna what ye mean,' said he; an wi that he gaed out intil the pend.
>
> Here anither servan-lass saw him an said tae the fowk staundin about,

'This chiel wis wi yon Nazaraean Jesus.'

Again Peter wadna tak wi it, but said wi an aith, 'I kenna the man!'

A wee after, the staunders-by gaed up til him an said, 'Ay, but ye war sae wi him, tae: your Galilee twang outs ye.'

At that he fell tae bannin an sweirin at he hed nae kennins o the man avà. An than a cock crew, an it cam back tae Peter hou Jesus hed said til him, 'Afore the cock craws, ye will disavou me thrice'; an he gaed out an grat a sair, sair greit.

I urge you to buy this great book. If my memory serves me well, Burgess remarked that he had never come across anybody like the Christ of the revised versions. But Lorimer's Christ he was familiar with. He was a real man, and he had often seen him in Glasgow pubs with a pint in his hand.

Ayrshire Words for Mayhem

An Ayrshire friend of mine has a splendid vocabulary of words for acts of mayhem. He is rather proud of this, but he insists that his words are in no way a reflection on the character of his nation. They merely prove the wonderful expressiveness of Scots when compared to anaemic southern English and Irish-English, he says. Wright's *English Dialect Dictionary* has all his words, in one form or another, and it sent me to look at a story called *The Brownie of Bodsbeck* by James Hogg, the Etterick Shepherd. In this tale of woe a herdsman is examined about some soldiers found slain.

'How did it appear to you that they had been slain? Were they cut with swords, or pierced with bullets?'

'I canna say, but they were sair hashed.'

'How do you mean?'

'Champit like, a' broozled and jurmumbled, as it were.'

'Do you mean that they, were cut, or cloven, or minced?'

'Na, na—no that ava. But they had gotten some sair doofs. They had been terribly paikit and daddid wi' something.'

'I do not in the least conceive what you mean.'

'That's extr'ord'nar, man. Can ye no understand folk's mither tongue?'

Hashed means bruised, ill-treated; *champit* means mashed, crushed: *broozled,* slashed. *Doof* is a violent blow from a club or some heavy weapon of that nature; *jurmumbled* means bespattered with blood; *paikit* means beaten severely; *daddit* means beaten to a bloody mess. All these words are still in use in Scotland, and in the north of Ireland.

That lovely word *fruition* has been paikit and doofit well and truly of late. I suppose people confused fruition with fruit, so that 'coming to fruition' was seen as 'coming to maturity'. But the word has nothing to do with fruit. It comes from the Late Latin *fruitio* enjoyment. There was a time when people knew how to use it properly. Christopher Marlowe has: 'That perfect bliss and sole felicity. The sweet fruition of an earthly crown.'

Coleridge was 'debarred the full fruition' of the use of tobacco by a sour physician. I'm afraid that the meaning of ripeness or maturity is now accepted by many dictionaries. But Oxford and Webster across the Atlantic, have so far given it the thumbs down.

Fockles and Brawse

Not a single child came to our door at Hallowe'en this year, a sign of the times I suppose. There was, however, a huge bonfire lit in the vicinity of our local pub; a host of children had gathered there, but their parents stood near, watchful. There, a man from west Limerick who has lived in our part of Wicklow for many years told me of the St John's Eve bonfires of his youth, and the huge torches they made, sheaves of straw fixed on long poles. They were an amazing sight in the darkness of his valley, he said, he hoped the custom was still in existence. These torches were called *fockles,* he told me. You didn't carry a torch for a girl, he went on; instead, she lit your fockle for you. The word was brought to Limerick by the Palatines. It is the German *fackel,* meaning a torch.

Mrs D. Kelly of Dundalk wants to know if *gansey* is an Irish word. Apart from hearing it used by ICA women all over the country, she came across the word in *Ulysses*: 'In workman's corduroy overalls, black gansy with red floating tie and apache cap.' The word is not Irish at all, although we are very fond of it; Beckett has it too, as has O'Flaherty and God knows how many more Irish writers. It has been assimilated into Irish, of course, as *geansaí,* but the word in all its forms is a dialect variant of *Guernsey.* It is used in Britain from Suffolk to Shetland, according to the English Dialect Dictionary.

A lady from Galway who, in her capacity as a social worker, has been collecting words from travelling people, sent me a beauty that mightn't go down well in the ICA. An overheard conversation went something like this: 'What age is Mongan's young wan now?' 'I don't know to hell. She's manable anyways.' My correspondent found that *manable* wasn't considered coarse by her informants; all that it implied was that she was of marriageable age. I have never heard the word used in Ireland, or, indeed, elsewhere; but the glossaries point out that this is impeccable Tudor English. 'She's manable,' says a character in Fletcher's *Maid In The Mill,* a good few years ago now.

Isn't it strange how words travel and survive, against all the odds? I recently read an account of hard times in Lancashire during William Cobbett's and Lord Ashley's campaign to help the wretched mill-children. The poor, when

they could get them, burned *brawse,* the account said—brambles and furze.
Brawse is none other than our Irish *breas*—glossed by Dinneen as 'a thicket,
a bush'.

Birds

A lady who lives near Clifden has kindly sent me a list of the local names of
a variety of birds. The list is very valuable to me; go raibh céad maith agat.
One of the birds is called locally the *crotach annagh,* and my reader says that
her father got as upset with a visiting French wild-fowler who shot one as
did the onlookers when the ancient mariner took the successful pot at the
albatross.

Yes. In one of Pearse's more doleful poems a mountainy woman says that
the death of her young son was foretold by the voices of the snipe and the
bird she calls the *crotach.* Now the crotach could have meant either the curlew
(*numenius arquata*) or the whimbrel (*numenius phaeopus*), also known as the
crotach eanaigh or marsh curlew, and I think this was the bird the poet—and
my Clifden friend—had in mind. The whimbrel, you see, can still put the
fear of God into people who live far from Pearse's beloved Conamara; I was
reminded of this a few years ago by an old sailor who lived in Arklow town.

He told me that the old people used to call the whimbrel the *Seven
Whistler,* as his screech is said to be repeated seven times. No ship would put
to sea in the old days if one of the sailors heard the bird, he assured me. This
bird of ill omen was also feared in England. *Notes and Queries* of 1871 tells
me that in Leicestershire 'the miners were in dread of hearing the warning
voice of the Seven Whistlers: birds sent, they say, by Providence to warn
them of an impending danger, and on hearing that signal not a man will
descend into the pit until he following day.' From Kent a correspondent
wrote to the editor of the English Dialect Dictionary: 'I never thinks any
good of them, there's always an accident when they comes. I never likes to
hear them.'

J. Sproule of Dunmurry, Belfast, asks what the origin of the words *stroop* and
scowler is. *Stroop,* he says, is the Antrim word for the gullet or windpipe. The
word is common all over the north; I've heard Donegal people talk of the stroop
of the teapot. It is of Scandinavian origin. Compare Swedish *strupe,* throat.

Scowder is glossed by Mr S. as an unqualified tradesman. A scowder is an
oaten cake, the outside only of which has been baked by being placed on
tongs laid over the embers. Hence my reader's figurative use of the word,
and Carleton's when he wrote in *Going to Maynooth.* 'He's but a scowder,
not a finished priest in the larnin.' It may be related to Old Norse *skorpna,*
to shrivel up. I'm guessing.

Panaydee, Wisha!

A lady from Leitrim wrote recently seeking information about a word common in her youth, but now fallen into disuse. The word is *panaydee*; the emphasis is on *ay*. It means what we used to call *goody* in Wexford, sweetened bread softened with hot milk, fed to children. My correspondent wants to know if the word is Irish.

No, it is of Spanish origin, I'm pretty sure, and it is to be found all over the north-west in one form or another. Peadar O'Donnell had it, as did Paddy the Cope. In Fermanagh it was pan*ah*dee and up in Inishowen it was recorded as *panada*. *Panada* is the Spanish for a mixture of flour, water, bread crumbs etc.

How then, did the word come to the north-west? I don't think we need look back to the time when that ungrateful scut, Capt Francisco de Cuellar swam ashore in Sligo from his Armada ship, and lived to call his Leitrim hosts *salvajes*—savages. A more likely source is the men who returned from Salamanca and other places of learning in subsequent centuries.

Claire Nyhan from Cork wants to know where we got *musha!* and *wisha!* These are euphemisms for *Muire*, the Blessed Virgin, just as Shakespeare's *marry!* is a euphemism for *Mary*. *Musha!* is Muire, nominative; *wisha!* is *a Mhuire*, vocative. John O'Keeffe is credited with being the first playwright to use wisha! It appears in the forgettable piece, *The She Gallant*, in 1767. Ben Jonson, as far as I know, was the first playwright to use a full-blown Irish swearing expression, in *New Inn*, circa 1629. An Irish nurse says *Er Grae Chreest!* (ar ghrá Chríost, for the love of Christ). From *grae* we may deduce that the lady spoke Ulster Irish. She followed this up with *Tower een cuppan D'usquebagh doone!* (Tabhair aon chupán d'uisce beatha dúinn—Give us one cup of whiskey). Ben made a better fist of Irish than did his pal from Warwickshire.

Mary Harrington writes from Cobh, and she asks whether *coach*, the person who trains athletes individually, is related to *coach*, the upmarket wagon. Nobody is sure, but I think it reasonable that the person who coached athletes was seen to give his pupils a lift, so to speak, or to carry them. At any rate, the fancy wagon got its name through Middle French *coche,* from *Kocs,* the Hungarian village where coaches were first made. I am reminded of an old *Punch* cover depicting a rowing eight getting plastered at a riverside inn, while their mentor sat disconsolate in the car park, under a sign that proclaimed: Sorry! Positively No Coaches.

Strap and Fiasco

A few weeks ago I heard the word *strap* applied to a stubborn pig by a Wexford lady of the soil.

Strap is Irish, a slightly modified version of *straip*, which Dinneen defines as a harlot. The more restrained O Dónaill has 'a vixen'. A late 17th century manuscript called *Purgatorium Hibernicum* has this: 'Amongst this traine, who (thinke you) espied he/But his old mistress, Madam Dydy?—/That pin'd to death, the fawneing strapp!/Some say for love, some of a clapp.'

Lover uses the word in *Handy Andy:* 'You infernal old strap!, shouted he, as he clutched a handful of bottles on the table near him, and flung them at the nurse'. Joyce used the word in Molly Bloom's soliloquy: '. . . you be damned you lying strap'; and more recently, Tom Murphy, in *Bailegangaire*, has 'Pat went back to his strap of a widdy. An' was dead in six months.' The word is not in use across the water.

Lover's bottle-firing gentleman brings me back to the troublesome *fiasco*. Mr Charles Acton, who knew a thing or two about music, solved the problem, I feel. He told me that in the last century, when an operatic performance did not please the gods of the Italian opera houses, they were inclined to fling their *fiaschi* at the performers. I can imagine how the word *fiasco,* a bottle, was transferred to describe a performance which merited a belt of one across the lug. Dr Máire Egan, another eminent musicologist, told me that Rossini once promised to let his mother know how a first-night went. He did so by sending her a card on which there were no words, just a drawing of a wine bottle: a fiasco, mammy, I'm afraid. I hope this explanation satisfies Mr Cecil Bell of Sutton, who brought the matter up last year.

Husbands and Other Matters

Where in Ireland does the word *husband* mean a *wife*? In the parish of Magherawarden, in Donegal, according to H.C. Hart, who recorded it in the dying years of the last century. 'A woman there said to a gentleman friend of mine', wrote Hart, 'I hear you and your husband are parted. He said, 'Wife, you mean, I suppose?' 'Well', she said, 'we call it the husband.' My friend said, 'Is that because she generally manages the house?' but she could give no answer.

Hart was right in thinking that the old lady was using the word husband in the archaic sense of 'the manager of a household'. 'Borrowing dulls the edge of husbandry', wrote the man from Stratford, and in his day husbandry was the business of the wife.

When I appealed to readers of this column almost two years ago for dialect words which I could include in a dictionary of the English we speak in Ireland, I had no idea that the response would be so great. Words which must be of Irish origin, but which I cannot find in the dictionaries, have turned up in the net. From Laois comes the word *cawmer*. The sentence Mary Gladney gives is 'the bale fell on his head, but he picked himself up without a cawmer on him'. Is *cawmer* related to the Irish *cáim*, blemish?

From a Westmeath reader came *brillem*, a fight, rumpus, and *kimayres*, silly antics. Where do these words have their origin? These two words were published in the learned journal *Éigse*, in 1948 by Eamon Mac an Fhailigh, under *bruilleam* and *ciméar*, Mrs Seery, but as you say in your part of Westmeath, he, too, was at an *amplish* to know where they came from. *Aimpléis* means trouble, difficulty. Long may these good words live in Moygoish and beyond.

Old Dublin Words

Mr John Wilde Crosbie, writing from the Law Library, referred to the old Donegalman's use of *husband* when he meant a wife, and to the word's original Tudor usage. A less archaic example is the use of the term *ship's husband,* he points out. The Merchant Shipping Act of 1894 provided that 'where there is not a managing owner there shall be registered the name of the ship's husband or other person to whom the management of the ship is entrusted'. Alas, Mr Crosbie tells me, the lovely old term has been deleted from our Irish law books. 'When Irish ships were legislated for in 1955, the Irish parliamentary draughtsman dropped the words *ship's husband* in favour of the word *person*. It would seem, therefore, that British ships can have a husband while Irish ships cannot. Ship-owning has surely become less romantic as a result'. Amen to that.

Mr Chalmers Trench of Killrian, Slane, Co. Meath, has sent me a veritable treasury of old words, some of which he has collected himself, the others noted by his father, W.F. Trench of TCD, in the early thirties, from his housekeeper, Mrs Hammersley, who came of Dublin Protestant working-class stock. Here is Trench senior: 'Across from my gate is the entrance to a public park into which a neighbour takes a spaniel every morning, and my alsatian goes over to play with him. One day Mrs H. told me that the spaniel turned up at our gate in the morning looking for the alsatian—'he came to give him the ban, that they were to be in the park at an earlier hour.' We know *banns* (plural only) of wedding announcements, and ban as a curse or proclamation. Neither of these can be in question here. Mrs H. had used the word in its original sense, a summons by public proclamation, chiefly, in early use, a summons to arms or to a tourney. Thus the word was a faultless

choice . . . the latest time at which the word is known to have been used
in writing in any such sense was circa 1450.'

Mrs H. also used the old verb *to reave*. She was referring to using a special
carpet-sweeper on a hand-made, thick-pile carpet. She said *to reave* meant to
pull the pile out. This 'obsolete and rare word', the OED says, was not
recorded after 1643. She referred to a potato pit, as a *bing*. This is an old
Norse word for, simply, a heap. She called a suspension balance an *auncel,* a
word of the 17th century and no later, according to the OED; and on
occasions she called the cat *faggot*. No! It was, she said, a term of abuse applied
to a woman.

Bonefires and Banjaxed

John Ross, who wrote to me from far-away Melbourne, tells me that he is
flummoxed. The cause of his woe is that he isn't sure whether to say *bonfire*
or *bonefire*. Born and reared in Co. Mayo, he never heard *bonfire* in his life
until he was sent to boarding school in Dublin, where his pronunciation was
'corrected'.

Bonfire is the version you'll find in the dictionaries nowadays, I'm afraid.
Dr Johnson claimed that it came from French *bon* + fire, 'a fire made for
some public cause or triumph'. Other etymologists have said that the word
comes from the Danish, *baum*, a beacon; and a Welshman of my acquaintance
swears that it is related to the Welsh *ban*, high. Still others find a relationship
with Anglo Saxon *bael*, fire, from *bael*, burning, and point to Icelandic *bal*,
flame, whence, the English *bale*, harm.

I think you can dismiss all these with a baleful smirk. *Bonfire is* merely a
softening of *bonefire,* and although this has long been accepted, you'll find
some people still arguing that the word referred to the great pyres of the
bones of victims of the medieval European plagues, or possibly to the victims
of religious persecution burned at the stake. The earliest written reference
to the fire, in an ecclesiastical tract of 1483, has *banefyre*, glossed as *ignis ossium*,
a fire of bones.

But why bones? Because under the feudal laws timber was not available
to the poor in winter, and bones from the shambles were the only substitute
available, especially to those who lived in towns. *Banefire* is the variant still
used in Durham; we find *bonefire* used all over rural England still, and, indeed
all over Ireland. And we got it right in Irish when we called the thing *tine
cnámh*.

Where, asks Mary Grace from Kilkenny, does *banjax* come from? It is in
all probability original Dublin slang. Flann O'Brien has it in *At Swim-Two-
Birds* (1939): 'Here is his black heart sitting there as large as life in the middle
of the pulp of his banjaxed corpse.' Beckett used it in *Waiting for Godot* in

the 1956 edition: 'Lucky might get going all of a sudden. Then we'd be banjaxed.' But in the 1954 edition of the play he used the word *ballocksed* instead. I wonder why he changed things. I see that a reader of this column, Mr Terence Wogan, has found everlasting fame in having his name associated with *banjaxed* in the new OED. 'I am out to banjax the bookies,' said he on BBC radio in 1979. I hope he succeeded.

Paddyisms?

Jo Brierley, who lives in London's Holland Park, asks me to settle an argument, or rather two arguments. She wants to know if the phrases 'the top of the morning' and 'broth of a boy' are genuinely Irish. 'They sound stage-Irish', she says, 'and whether they are or not I detest them because most English people think they are Paddyisms'.

To judge from the frequency with which it was used in English hunting literature in the 18th century, 'the top of the morning to you' is as English as cakes and ale. It was an expression of thanks on being offered a stirrup cup; and as such John Surtees's Mr Sponge used it in the 19th century. But that said, it became widely used as a civil greeting far from the exciting atmosphere of lawn meets, in Scotland and Ireland as well as England. Samuel Lover was the first to use the phrase in our literature, back in 1848, as far as I know; but I blame the Boston-based John Boyle O'Reilly for spreading the expression through nationalist Ireland when he bade Ireland, which he found looking grand, the top of the morning in a popular sentimental poem.

As for 'broth of a boy', it seems to be an Ulster phrase, and William Carleton was, I think, the first to have used it in print, in *Traits and Stories* (1843): 'As he was a broth of a boy at dancing, the servants would strike up a dance in the kitchen.' It was not, as far as I am aware, recorded outside of Ireland in the 19th century.

But why broth? I don't really know. You'd have found some interesting brothy phrases in use across the water in Victoria's time. 'I'll blaw her broth for her' meant 'I'll give her a scolding,' in Yorkshire. 'To warm up old broth' meant 'to renew acquaintance with an old flame' in Lincolnshire; 'a great broth of sweat' meant 'a heavy perspiration' in Scotland.

Voteen is a word Mrs Joan McGowan heard her mother, who came from Cavan, use in her youth. By it she meant a crawthumper. It comes from *devotee,* possibly through some cognate Irish word like *deabhóidín,* which sounds derisory. Carleton has *voteen,* too: 'Up near the altar . . . you might perceive a voteen, repeating some new prayer or choice piece of devotion.' But the word is not confined to the north. Patrick Kennedy has it in *The Banks of the Boro* (1869), that fine book about Co. Wexford. He said that a certain man was one of the class that is called in Scotland 'the unco guid', and 'voteens' among ourselves.

Moll Doyle

I met a man in a Kildare hostelry recently who told me that he had the good sense, 40 odd years ago, to marry a Wexford woman. 'Did you ever', he asked me, 'try to get a stubborn sow into a sty?' I confessed that I never had to perform this delicate manoeuvre. 'Well', he said, 'the missus says on occasions like that, "Get in you strap of hell, or I'll give you Moll Doyle".' Who is, or was, Moll Doyle? he wanted to know. I promised to find out.

During the 18th and early part of the 19th century various secret societies for the redress of agrarian grievances flourished. They were often said to be under the command of a leader, generally fictitious, with a fanciful name such as Lady Clare or, in Co. Wexford, our friend Moll Doyle. The rank-and-file of the parties who committed outrages at night were known as Moll Doyle's Daughters. P.W. Joyce tells us that 'by the powers of Moll Doyle!' was a harmless oath that outlived the agrarian troubles. Patrick Kennedy, in his fine account of mid-Wexford life, *The Banks of the Boro* (1867), has this: 'Some folk, however, owed him a spite for the taking of the land, and Moll Doyle and her daughters were hired to pay him a visit.' 'Don't mention my name,' implored my Kildareman, 'or she'll give *me* Moll Doyle!' Understood.

J. Bell from Bangor, tells me that in his (?) youth kids used to play a game called *neevy navy nick nack,* and wonders whether the game was confined to the north of Ireland.

I think I've heard my friend, David Hammond, speak of this. (You may remember his beautiful television programme on the street games of Belfast, *Dusty Bluebells*). Wright's English Dialect Dictionary has quite a long piece about this game. Apparently it was popular across the water in both Scotland and England as well as in the north of Ireland. Says Wright: 'Some small article, such as a marble or a sweet is put into one hand secretly. The boy then comes up to a companion with both hands closed, and cries, as he revolves the two fists before his friend's eyes, *nievey, nievey nick nack, which hand will ye tak? Tak the right, tak the wrang, I'll beguile ye if I can.* The fun is in the challenged person choosing the hand in which there is nothing.' *Nievie* is a variant of that old dialect word *neive*. It comes from the Old Norse *hnefi,* which also means a fist. It was once common in all the Viking strongholds of Ireland. Maybe Moll Doyle used it.

Queens and Queans

A reference I made recently to the good old word *cotquean*, a man who is a little too interested in women's business, prompted a Kilkenny reader to ask whether the words *queen* and *quean* are related, and if they are, why they are spelled differently.

Queen and *quean* are very close relatives. *Queen* is from Old English *cwen*, related to Old Saxon *quan*, a wife. *Quean* is from Old English *cwene*, related to Old Saxon *quena*, a woman. But while *queen* has retained her regal status as a word, *quean* has descended to the brothel and the pub, except in Scotland and parts of the north of our own island, where Burns's *sonsie quean* would still be regarded as a fun-loving, good girl, not at all like the *queens* found in England. *Sonsie*, by the way is from the Gaelic *sonas*, happiness.

The English *quean* is a bad baggage, and she is found in many old plays, very often plying her trade in a tavern. There was never any confusion with *queen*, as Byron showed when he applied the term *queen of queans* to a wanton shrew.

Wanton? I must be careful. Here we have another word with a variety of meanings. The 13th-century source word was *wantowen*, ungovernable unruly, which was what I had in mind when I wrote 'wanton shrew'. The beautiful word *wanton* came to be used in two contradictory senses quite early in its life, and by Shakespeare's time a wanton was a quean. You may remember the dark lady in *Love's Labour's Lost* —'A whitely wanton with a velvet brow./With two pitch balls stuck in her face for eyes./Ay, and by heaven, one that will do the deed/Though Argus were her eunuch and her guard.'

But the innocent, sinless wanton, reflecting the state of nature, existed too. Listen to Friar Lawrence: 'Here comes the lady: O, so light a foot/Will ne'er wear out the everlasting flint;/A lover may bestride the gossamer/That idles in the wanton summer air/And yet not fall; so light is vanity.'

In Herrick's day wanton came to mean wandering, and God knows how many poets wrote of wanton rivers and streams. Even the great Milton could be carried away when writing about them. Apart from being wanton, the Severn, a *quean* among rivers (in the English sense) in my humble opinion, was, according to John, 'glassie, translucent and and coral-paven'. Maybe she was in his day, but on the other hand, the poor man's sight was never too good.

Middlebrows and Musebrows

I have often wondered why the estimable Master Desmond Keogh uses the word *middlebrow* to describe people who listen to his excellent radio programme. Collins describes middlebrow as a disparaging word for a person with conventional tastes and limited cultural appreciation. Not at all the type of person who tunes in to *Music for Middlebrows*. I suppose the word was coined not long after the introduction of *highbrow* and *lowbrow* during the Great War: these are Americanisms, according to Eric Partridge. Highbrow, Bernard Shaw said, is a person educated beyond his intelligence.

There used to be a *musebrow* too, and this seems to have come into short-lived fashion with the publication of Elizabeth Barrett Browning's *Sonnets from the Portuguese*. EBB wrote of her loved one's poetic lock, offered as a gift: 'As purply black as erst to Pindar's eyes/The dim purpureal tresses gloomed athwart/The white Muse-brows.'

Muse-brow here means no more than the brow of the Muse, but the young Victorian ladies who had just been introduced to the passionate sonnets of the lady from Wimpole Street used the word to describe anybody who fitted their notion of what a poet should look like—a highbrowed cove with a shock of unruly black hair. In no time at all, however, *musebrow* had become a term of contempt for the type of *cotquean* Mrs B. herself described in *Aurora Leigh*: 'There are men/Born tender, apt to pale at a trodden worm./Who paint for Pastime, in their favourite dream,/Spruce auto-vestments flowered with crocus-flames.'

The word *cotquean* has become obsolete and more's the pity; English hath need of it. It meant originally a cottage woman, but by Shakespeare's time it had come to mean a man who poked his nose into what women then regarded as their business. You may remember the scene in *Romeo and Juliet* in which Capulet is trying to hurry up the preparations for the wedding feast. The Nurse tells him that the business of the kitchen is none of his. 'Go, you cotquean go,' she orders.

Restoration comedy also has *cotquean* as a term of mockery for this type of male busybody. He is usually mocked, not by the men but by the women and called *chuck* by them, to add insult to injury. Macbeth called his wife *chuck*, you'll remember. *Chuck* is chicken. Some chicken.

Fortnail, Shool, and a Tudor Survival

Flann Ó Riain has sent me the word *fortnail*, which is used not alone in the lovely Tipperary glen he lives in, but in south Kilkenny as well, where it is pronounced *forneeal*, with the emphasis on *nee*. It means a small egg. Dinneen has it under *fóirnéall* and he gives the variants *fóirtnéal* and *fuairtnéal*. It is glossed by him as 'an inconspicuous object'. Hence, Dinneen points out, 'níl ann ach fóirnéall' means 'it (the egg) is very small'. Delighted to have the word.

Another word I had not come across before in the English of Ireland is *shool*. A man from Ballycastle, Co. Antrim, sent me this word, which he heard used by a young man on his way home from school. 'I got out of there', the garsún confided to a friend, 'like shit from a shoot'. *Shool is* an old dialect word for shovel and Wright's great dialect dictionary of 1898 shows that it was then common in Ireland. *Shool* is still known in Donegal, I'm told. 'I'm going to shool the street' means to the older people who live at the back of Muckish, 'I'm going to shovel the dirt from the space in front of the house,' not 'I'm going to walk the road,' as you might think. Joseph Wright gives us some phrases, one of which is a laundered version of the Antrim scholar's pungent one: *like shot out of a shool*—with great speed. I can't imagine a wildfowler using a shovel by way of a shotgun. Two other phrases were: *the sexton has shaked his shool at him*—he is unlikely to recover from his illness.

Something I wrote about Tudor survivals in Irish English some weeks ago prompted John Walsh from Waterford to remind me of a beauty noted by Archbishop Sheehan of Melbourne in Ring parish, and explained by the late R.B. Breatnach in *Seana-Chaint na nDéise 2*. The term was *gad seang* also found in the form *gad sanns,* and used in the phrase *Dh'éiri sé ar a ghad seang chugam,* which, translated literally, would mean the nonsensical 'He got up on his narrow withe to me'. *Gad seang* is a corruption of the English asseveration *zounds* (God's wounds), and originally the Irish phrase would have meant something like 'he started to use zounds! or God's wounds! when he addressed me'. In other words, he got up on his high horse.

I was both amazed and delighted recently to find that so many of the Irish words collected by Archbishop Sheehan over 70 years ago still live on in the rich English of west Waterford.

Mismanners and Other 'Mis' Words

In the absence of a dictionary of the English we speak in Ireland we musn't blame the OED for telling us that the noun, plural, *mismanners,* meaning bad manners, has been obsolete since 1820. I heard it myself not a stone's throw from the town of sweet Dungloe last summer, and in deepest Wexford, near Tacumshane, only last week.

Irish English has retained some very interesting words prefixed by *mis*. *Mismoved* is one. It means worried, upset. Shakespeare has it, and so has Seumus MacManus of Donegal, who has this passage in *In Chimney Corners*, published in 1899: 'Good morra,Willie, says he with an ugly smile on his face as much as to say "I'm goin' to get even with ye at last, boy-o". "Good morra, and good luck," says Willie, not the laist thrifle mismoved, seemin.'

Another northern word, recorded by Traynor, is the verb *mismorrow*. It means to take some article by mistake, thinking it was one's own. 'I mismorrowed the hat'. *Morrow* itself is interesting. It is both a noun and a verb. As a noun, it means a match, equal. '*That's* not the morrow of *that*', I

once heard a Cavan-born teacher point out to a pupil who was having trouble
with an equation. According to the English Dialect Dictionary, in Tyrone
and Donegal the verb *to morrow* means 'to borrow a horse for the day on the
understanding that one lends a horse in return the next day'.

Mishanter is another borrowing from Scots. It means bad luck, mischance.
'I drove into the loch by mishanter' explained a driver to a Donegal court a
few years back. In the north *misdoubt*, verb and noun, can mean many things.
As a verb it can mean to disbelieve. 'I don't misdoubt you' is still common.
It also means to suspect, or fear. 'I misdoubt greatly there'll be rain, was
recorded by H.C. Hart in Fanad. As a noun *misdoubt* means a suspicion, a
doubt. 'I have a misdoubt that all's not right up there'.

Misgiggle is another beauty. It means to upset, spoil. 'Marriages are made
in heaven, but a lot of them are misgiggled on the way down', said a wise
man to Traynor. Finally, there's the verb *to mislippen*. It's what the Department of Education is reportedly doing to the English Leaving Cert. syllabus.
It means to mismanage, to overlook, to shamefully neglect something or
somebody. I'm thinking of William Shakespeare.

Pregnant Pauses

'I have often wondered how the phrases *pregnant pause* and *pregnant silence*
came into the language,' writes a Dublin doctor. He goes on: 'Is there any
relationship between the *pregnant* in those phrases and the word which means
carrying a foetus in the womb?' A darlin' question, doctor, and one often
ignored by the major dictionaries. Collins, for example, says that the root of
pregnant is the Latin *praegnans*, from *prae,* before, and *(g)nasci,* to be born.
Correct as far as the obstetric term goes; but in relation to pregnant pauses
and silences, there must be a doubt.

There was a second *pregnant* in English in days gone by. It was used to
describe abstract concepts. It means urgent, weighty, compelling. The
Tudors knew it. Shakespeare has Iago use it in *Othello*. When trying to
discredit Cassio, Othello's right-hand man, he says to Roderigo: 'Now, sir,
this granted, as it is a most pregnant and unforced position, who stands so
eminently in the degree of this fortune as Cassio does?' It was used in Scotland
until the 19th century. Sir Walter Scott has: 'One of the constables, besides
the pregnant proof already produced, offers to make oath'. This archaic
pregnant came from Old French *pregnant,* ultimately from Latin *premere* to
press. It is, I think, the word which survives in pregnant silences and pauses.

Mrs Mary Maher, who hails from near Nenagh, says that in her part of
the world a cantankerous old woman is sometimes called a *baggage*. She
wonders why. It is in English since the 15th century and it came from Old
French *bagage,* from *bague,* a bundle, which in turn may have come from Old

Norse, *baggi*, bag. But how did a word for luggage come to mean a cantankerous old woman here in Ireland; a prostitute, a saucy young woman, and a woman of no account in England? The camp followers travelled with the wagons in old God's time. These were the baggage women. There were all kinds to be found among them, and this fact gave rise to the variety of glosses on *baggage* from 1500 onwards. Shakespeare used baggage in Mrs Maher's sense in the *Taming of the Shrew*. Christopher Sly was called a rogue and he answered: 'Y'are a baggage: the Slys are no rogues'. Baggage in this sense is not confined to Tipperary; it is to be found in many places colonised in the 17th century.

Cards and Card-playing Terms

C. Boyle, of Letterkenny, has sent me some interesting words connected with cardplaying. In rural east Donegal, he tells me, the joker is called the *nabs*, the ten of clubs is *Mooney's apron*, *Conn* is the ace of diamonds. Another expression he has heard is '*fáinne óir on anybody?*'—has anybody got the gold ring? The *fáinne óir* is the ace of hearts. A person who wins a trick with the ace of hearts in '25' shouts 'The cock's in the long meadow!' I wonder why.

Jane King, from Furryhilll, Rathmore, near Naas, has heard the term *murrin ditch*, meaning a boundary ditch, in her part of the world. This is a variant of the old dialect word *mearing*, also found as *mearn* and *mering*. It means a boundary, as does the older noun, *mear*, sometimes spelled *meer*. In the days before the introduction of enclosures boundaries between common fields or between different properties were shown by balks or strips of grass.

These old words, for some reason discarded by most of the major dictionaries and found only in dialect lexicons, are still used by country people all over England, Scotland and Ireland. *Meer* is glossed as a *marke be-twene ij londys* in a glossary written in Chaucer's time. Spenser has: '*And Hygate made the meare thereof by West*' in the *Faery Queene*. *Meer, mearing,* and the Kildare *murrin* come from the Old English *gemære*, a boundary.

Molly Bloom's Budget

No doubt about it: J.F. Killeen of Galway has solved the problem of Molly Bloom's *budget*. He must share the sweets with Eoin C. Bairéad of Kenilworth Park, Dublin, who has also pointed out to me that *budget* here means a paper or magazine, and that Joyce had used the word earlier in the book when he has J.J. O'Mulloy say: 'Ignatius Gallaher we all know and his Chapelizod boss, Harmsworth of the farthing press, and his American cousin of the Bowery gutter sheet not to mention *Paddy Kelly's Budget, Pue's Occurrences* and our watchful friend the *Skibbereen Eagle.*'

Paddy Kelly's paper, sub-titled 'A Pennyworth of Fun', was the only paper calling itself a budget that was published in Ireland between 1800 and the time of Poldy's ramble. Its editor was Alfred Howard, pseudonym Paddy Kelly, and it flourished in the 1830s. It was immensely popular with Dubliners and its motto was 'to give entertainment to all, information to many, offence to none. It published light verse, stories, local news and gossip, jokes and puzzles.

But why budget? It simply meant a sack or bag. I am reminded of Séamus Heaney's and Ted Hughes's anthology, *Rattlebag*, and the 18th-century Irish *Bolg an tSoláthair*, a miscellany of prose and/or verse, such as the one the library of TCD has in its keeping, a manuscript lovingly transcribed by a James O'Fergusa in 1702. It is extraordinary that *budget*, a waver full of tidbits of all kinds, and the *bolg* (an tsoláthair) of the 18th and 19th centuries both come from the same source, through the Latin *bulga*, from a Celtic word meaning a bag.

Thanks too, to Eamon Maher of Gortmuller, Roscrea, to Michael Knightly of Doneraile, and to R. Dunne of Portmarnock, for telling me that a knapsack sprayer is called a *budget* in many parts of Ireland.

Jane King, from Furry Hill, Rathmore, Naas, tells me that a neighbouring farmer refers to the microscopic insects that infest hay as *fenians*. Nothing to do with Finn or the 1867 revolutionaries, this, but most likely a corruption of *fineog*, Irish for microbe.

Latchikoes and Policasters

Professor Richard Wall is a noted Joycean scholar, author of *An Anglo-Irish Dialect Glossary for Joyce's Works*. He teaches at the University of Calgary in Canada and wrote to this column hoping that I might be able to shed some light on the origin and exact meaning of one of the most unusual words he has encountered in an Irish text: *latchiko*. He first came across it in the *Letters of. . .* series of John B. Keane, and was inclined to dismiss it as a nonce word, that is a word coined for a single occasion. It is pejorative, as is clear from the context in which it appears: 'Then there's that depraved git, the Land-For-All latchiko, Joey Connors.' Recently he encountered the word in *Petticoat Loose*, a play by the Galwayman, M.J. Mulloy. In this work it is consistently used for a changeling: '. . . it's fairy latchicoes that die, while the real babies live on in the forts, if they aren't charmed back.'

Latchiko seems to be in general use in the south of Ireland and I've heard it said that it originated on the building sites of England. It means 'a conniving, untrustworthy, backstabbing sleeveen', according to a retired

London bricklayer I have the occasional pint with. Neither he nor I can even hazard a guess as to its origins.

Mr R.J. Blakenay of Bangor, Co. Down, wants to know the origin of *wag,* meaning a jocular fellow. His Collins says that it is of uncertain origin. Does it come from tongue-wagger, he asks. No, it comes, according to the excellent *World Book Dictionary,* from the obsolete *waghalter,* a person likely to *wag* on the gallows. *Wag* itself comes from Middle English *waggen,* from root of Old English *wagian,* to move backwards and forwards.

Miss J. Fitzgerald from Waterford wants to know the origin of the suffix in *poetaster,* a writer of inferior verse. The *aster* bit was a late Latin diminutive suffix to *poeta.* It also survived in such words as *rhymester* and Dr Johnson's rare *policaster,* which he defined as 'A petty, ignorant pretender to politicks'— one of that prattling, importunate class on which a redoubtable lady puts manners in television's Prime Time. Shakespeare foresaw our *policasters,* I'd swear. You may remember Viola in *Twelfth Night:* 'Holla your name to the reverberate hills/ And make the babbling gossip of the air/ Cry out, "Olivia!" '

Donegal Words

From Mrs Anne MacMenamin who hails from Fanad, Co. Donegal, and who now lives in Boston, comes a query about a word used in Fanad in her youth. The word is *hirsle,* and it means 'to mooch along in an aimless manner', she says. Traynor's dictionary has it as a variant of *hissel.* Other variants collected by him are *hersle* and *hurstle.* One of his informants defined the word as 'to move in a creeping or trailing manner', and H.C. Hart, whose glossary Traynor used, has 'to move something with much friction of effort, as a heavy sack or barrel'. Another correspondent of Traynor's, the Rev. C.W. Quin of Moville, added: 'A drunken man lying in a ditch, when offered help said: I hirselled in be mesel, an' be mesel I'll hirsle oot again.'

The word hirselled in to Donegal from Scotland, and it is an old word, with many relatives, one of which is the good old Scots noun *hushloch,* hurried, careless, slovenly work; also a slovenly person, untidy in dress. Another relative is the compound *hushel-bushel,* an uproar, and *hushly,* disordered, dishevelled.

Douglas, it seems was the first to use *hirsel* in print, away back in 1513: 'For on blind stannis . . . hirssilit we.' It is of Scandinavian origin. Compare the Danish *ryste,* to shake, and the Old Norse *hyrsta.*

Another interesting Donegal word of Scandinavian origin is *Katirams,* small, swift-moving clouds that are said to presage an Atlantic storm. I first heard the word used by Donegal trawlermen sheltering far from home in Dunmore East. *Katirams* comes, I'm pretty sure, from Old Norse *kottr,* cat and *ramr*, fierce. But Traynor taking his cue from the English Dialect Dictionary says it comes from Norwegian dialect *katt*, cat and *ramm*, a paw. Take your pick.

Hoke is a Donegal word that, because of its association with the tatties, has become famous. To hoke of course, means to dig, root, scrape out. It is also spelled *holk* and *howk* in Scotland, and is in use for a long time. To *holke* was explained as to work with a *pala* (Latin, spade) in 1485. Again, there is a Scandinavian connection: compare Swedish *hålka*, to make hollow.

Norse Words from the South-East

A commonly used word in south-east Wexford is *hylin'*, meaning raining heavily. Its origin was a mystery to me until a letter arrived from Mr J. Walsh of Waterford City asking about a local expression, *hailin'*, which also means raining cats and dogs. *Hylin'* and *hailin'* are the same word, I'm sure. Neither has anything to do with the word for those nasty small pellets of ice we are all too familiar with; that *hail* comes from Old English *hægl*, related to Greek *hakhlex*, pebble.

The verb *hale*, also written *hail*, is in common use from the Scottish border to Dorset. It can mean to pour, to empty out, as water from a vessel by inclining it to one side. It also means to flow, to run down in a large stream; to pour. In the Bellenden *Livy* of 1533 we find *the teris began fast to hale ower hir chekis*; and in one of the Child *Ballads* we find *Drops of blude frae Rose the Red Came hailing to the groun'*. The English Dialect Dictionary records the phrase *the sweat hales of'n me o'nights* from Scotland, and also tells us that the phrases *its hailin' on* and *Hailin' down* are commonly used with respect to a heavy rain.

How did this come into use in Waterford and Wexford? It is legacy from the hard men who came to visit on the long ships. *Halla* is the Old Norse for to lean, to tilt, to turn sideways so as to pour.

Two other words of Norse origin came my way recently. The first was sent to me by an angler from Graiguenamanagh who heard the word used by prime boys who used to poach salmon in the far off days when the king of fish was plentiful in the Barrow. The word is *leester*, and law-abiding anglers like my correspondent would know it as an illegal type of gaff. The English Dialect Dictionary has it as *leister*, and it quotes a bit from Queen Victoria's Journal: 'All our tenants were assembled with poles or spears, or rather leisters, for catching salmon.' It comes from, Old Norse *ljostr*, a salmon spear.

And lastly the old verb, *hain*, which means to use wisely, sparingly. 'Hain at the brim and you'll hae at the bottom' is an excellent piece of canny northern advice. I wonder is the word to be found in the south? It may well have survived: it is to be found in many parts of England as well as Scotland. It comes from the Old Norse *hegna*, to protect, preserve, enclose with a fence or hedge. Thanks to J.B.S. of Enniskillen for the word and for the nice letter.

Can-can

I have often wondered where the French got their expressive *can-can*, the high-kicking dance of the Parisian cafés. Mr John Roche from Waterford is wondering about the word as well. The major French and English dictionaries are not very helpful, Larousse, Collins and Oxford, for example, playing safe with 'of uncertain origin'. The *World Book Dictionary* is prepared to hazard a guess. 'Probably from a childish pronunciation of *canard*, duck, from the dance steps that resemble a duck's waddle', it says. Indeed? Well now, maybe I went to the wrong cafés, but the two can-cans I saw in my youth while engaged in scholarly research in Pigalle in no way resembled a duck's waddle. I like this explanation from an anonymous glossary of French slang, written when Toulouse-Lautrec and the can-can were the talk of Paris. 'This lascivious dance is named from the learned discussions that nightly take place outside the cafés of Montparnasse, the haunt of university scholars. These gentlemen are wont to qualify their loud arguments with the Latin *quamquam* (although), and from it the students who eavesdrop on them and make fun of them have coined a word, pronounced *con-con,* which has by now become a part of demotic Parisian French, a term for nonsense. The students have also made a bawdy pun on the sound of the word and have named the lewd and wanton dance from it.' There you are. I'm not asking you to believe it.

A Baltinglass reader quoted me a snatch of a local ballad written sometime in the last century according to the broadside evidence. The young lady praised in the song was said to be 'fairer than Hypatia bright, and free from earthly pride,/A comely maid, and her dwelling place lay near to the tanyard side'. Who, my correspondent asks, was Hypatia?

A sad story, this. According to the *Oxford Classical Dictionary* she was a noble lady, learned in mathematics, and philosophy. She died in AD 415. A daughter of the mathematician Theon of Alexandria, she revised some of her father's works, and went on to become influencial as a teacher of the pagan Neoplatonist philosophy. She was torn to pieces by a mob of Christians, some say on the instigation of their bishop, Cyril, who later became, after a singular reformation, Saint Cyril of Alexandria, defender of the unity of Christ's person, divine and human, against Nestorius at the Council of Ephesus.

Poor Hypatia. I'm glad she has found fame of a kind in Baltinglass.

Scalteen

That noted, traveller from Prussia, Prince Hermann Ludwig Heinrich von Pückler-Muskau, was introduced to the Irish beverage *scalteen* after a hunt in Co. Tipperary, in the 1820s. It was served between courses, and the prince thought it was designed to sober one up. It had, of course, quite the opposite effect on him. I was reminded of this recently when the beverage was mentioned in a Wicklow hostelry by a man who told a chef who was in the company that he ought to add *scalteen* to his menu. Though I have frequently come across the word in the literature of the 19th century. I had never seen a reliable recipe for the brew. Fr Mathew denounced it in no uncertain terms, as did his friend, Mr MacNamara Downes from Clare, a very bad temperance poet who formed the rather unsuccessful Irish Water Drinkers' Association. *Scalteen* is the Irish *scailtín*; compare *scalladh*, burning, scalding, a burning sensation.

Mr Carl Duggan from Bray sent me to George A. Little's *Malachy Horan Remembers*. Said Malachy: 'They always had scalteen ready at Jobstown Inn. Men, in weather like this, out from morning till night without a bit, would be coming in with the mark of the mountain on them. Scalteen would make a corpse walk. It would put the life back in them, but make them drunk too. It was taken red hot. They made it from half a pint of whiskey, half a pound of butter, and six eggs. You should try it some time, but when you have it down, go to bed while are still able.'

Daniel O'Connell asked a witness during the trial of Fr Maguire in 1827 to define scalteen. The witness replied that it was a mixture of sugar, water and whiskey, boiled. 'Why, they call that punch,' said Dan. 'Not when the water is put down cold, and boiled with them,' replied the witness.

The problem is that the German prince's scailtín was a kind of consommé; and here, do chum glóire Thiobrad Árann, is a recipe sent to me by a man who identifies himself as 'somebody from Thurles who drinks now and again in Mary Willie's, and that should be enough for you'. This, he adds, is 'the greatest cure known to man for a cold or the flu'.

Add half a bottle of whiskey, two whisked eggs, a lump of butter, to a pint and a half water (or unsalted and strained beef broth) to which black pepper has been added. Boil the mixture. Consume.

Sláinte!

John Florio and His Dictionary

John Florio is one of the most attractive and amusing figures in English literary history. He was a Londoner born and bred, Italian by extraction, and his Italian-English Dictionary, dedicated to James the First's Queen, Anne of Denmark, was of great importance because it demonstrated to the myopic university asses of his (and Shakespeare's and Marlowe's and Jonson's) day that English could vie even with the admired Italian language for a rich, expressive and varied vocabulary. He loved words, and his brilliant translation of Montaigne's essays is another classic: as C.V. Wedgwood described it, it is as though a French watercolour had been enthusiastically copied in enamel.

In his dictionary, the handsome John, with whom, it was rumoured, the queen was in love, was rarely content to give one English version of an Italian word, but often gave two or three. This is how he glosses the lovely, onomatopaeic *sussarare*: 'To whisper to murmure. Also to humme or buzze as Bees. Also to charme or forspeake with whispering words. Also to make a low, a soft or still noise as a gentle winde among trees, or a gentle-gliding streame among pible-stones, or as birds chirping and chattering among woods'.

Here he is on some words ultimately derived from the Latin *femina*: '*Feminabile*: Weak, of a woman's nature. *Feminaccio*: A bawdie, womanish fellow. *Feminella*: A silly litle woman. *Feminetta*: A very litle pretty woman. *Feminina*: A very litle, litle woman.'

Florio's dictionary should be interesting to students of the history of medicine. *Climacterico* he says is 'the dangerous or perilous yeeres of ones life, commonly the year 63'. *Emontorij*, he informs us, are the 'kernelly places of the bodie by which the principall parts voide the superfluities, to wit, under the armes for the heart, under the eares for the braine, and under the share for the liuer.' (*Share* was a dialect word for coarse grass used in thatching.) *Fare il pano*, he says, is 'to die or kick up ones heeles and never to have more need of bread'. From *culare,* 'the arse', he throws in, in the fashion of our own Fr Dinneen, *culattorio*: 'a scoffing word, as one would say "the arserie of mankind" '.

John Florio's dictionary was published for his friend Anne in 1609. My (facsimile) copy was stolen from me recently. Alas it is long out of print.

Northern Words

What a rich mixture the English of the north of our fair island is. Mrs J. Gallagher of Letterkenny asks me whether I've heard the term *a draghy road*, meaning one that is deceptive in the sense that it is really longer than it appears to be. Traynor's glossary of Donegal English has it, and he thought it came from the Irish *bealach draíochta*, a magic (i.e. deceptive) road or way. The origin of the phrase *to lam*, meaning to beat, to thrash, puzzles her as well. She has never, she says, heard the phrase outside Donegal.

Lam is a common dialect or colloquial word, and is to be found all over Ireland, Britain and America, Mrs G. In my youth I used to go lamming for eels, thrashing the water so that the creatures would scurry into a net. 'Give him lam-and-holly' is an expression I've heard used by unscrupulous horse copers; 'lam-and-sally' is the English equivalent. This is a borrowing from our Scandinavian friends. Old Norse *lemja* meant to beat, thrash, flog. Old English has *lemian*, to lame any one, to break a horse.

A lady from the town of Strabane who wants to remain anonymous asks me whether I've ever heard the expression 'sailing around like marigolds in broth'. What a marvellously vivid expression it is. It is used in describing a young woman who fancies herself, says my correspondent. Apparently old people in the north west once used marigolds as a colouring and as a flavouring in *flummery*. That dish was a preparation of oatmeal offal. It was steeped in water and strained after a number of hours. The strainings were used as a substitute for milk. If left for a certain time they solidified somewhat into a kind of jelly. Flummery, my correspondent tells me, was a 'polite' word for *sowens*.

The word *distasted,* used to describe food gone off, spoiled, was common, according to Mr I.L. Campbell of Belfast, in rural Antrim, in his youth. Here we have a wonderful Tudor survival; you'll find it in one of the loveliest passages in Shakespeare, in which poor Troilus complains with heart-stopping poignancy of the hurried leave-taking that 'injurious time' has forced upon himself and Cressida: 'And scants us with a single famish'd kiss,/ Distasted with the salt of broken tears.'

False Etymologies

The late Eric Partridge had little time for those lexicographers who refused to hazard a guess as to the origin of a word, and perhaps this is why he usually spoke in a kindly way about people like Johnson and even Dr Brewer, author of the *Dictionary of Phrase and Fable*. Brewer rarely admitted defeat in chasing the history of a word and he could be mischievous in his magisterial pronouncements.

Take the word *charlatan*. The word comes from the Italian *ciarlatano*, from *ciarlare,* to prattle, clearly the safest refuge of a quack or an impostor whose lack of skill could be glossed over with a good smattering of jargon. Dr Brewer invented a French quack dentist named Latan who, he claimed, drove around Paris in a fancy carriage which he used as a mobile surgery. The sight of Latan, who wore flamboyant clothes, including a feathered Roman helmet, caused the phlegmatic citizenry to exclaim *Voilà le char de Latan!* he assures us.

But what is one to say of the blissful ignorance of John Ash, who published a dictionary in 1775? Mr Ash wasn't loath to steal other people's 'erudite etymologies' (the polite lexical euphemism for educated guesses) and he made plenty of use of Dr Johnson's dictionary. In doing so, however, he was apt to make a terrible ass of himself, as in the case of the word *curmudgeon*. Johnson defined the word as 'An avaricious, churlish fellow; a miser; a niggard' and he derived it as a corruption of *coeur méchant,* wicked heart. He credited this guess to 'Fr an unknown correspondent'. This gloss led poor John Ash astray. He credited Johnson with the discovery of the word's origin which, he assured his readers, was 'From the French *coeur,* unknown, and *méchant,* a correspondent'!

Such a good word as *curmudgeon* deserves a better pedigree than the 'of unknown origin' found in the major dictionaries. 'When in doubt check the dialects' is a good motto, and we find in the English Dialect Dictionary, from the Shetlands and Orkney, *curmullyit,* a dark, ill-favoured fellow; and *curmuring,* a low rumbling or murmuring, an echoic word from the neighbours in Scotland.

Are these words akin to *curmudgeon?* I think so.

Country Words

Mr James Ferguson, who farms in Co. Down, asks whether farmers in the south have the word *rowen* in their vocabulary. It means the second crop of hay. I have never heard the word, but the English Dialect Dictionary tells me it is found all over our neighbouring island in various forms: *rowen, rouen, rawings, rawn* and *rowins,* to mention but a few. *Rowen,* then, is the *aftermath,* another old farming word that has survived; still another term for it is *lattermath.* But in places they make a fine distinction between *rowen* and the other two words: in Lincolnshire, when the second crop of grass is eaten on the land it is called *lattermath* and *aftermath;* when mown and made into hay, it is termed *rowen.* Rowen comes from *rewayn,* from Old French. *Aftermath,* a 16th-century word, comes from after + *math,* a mowing, from Old English *mæð.* Rowen is also a 16th-century word. In 1523 the bookkeeper of St John's Hospital in Canterbury recorded that he had 'rec. of Cady for the rowen gras xiiij.d.'

Anne Sherry, who comes from Magheracloon, outside Carrickmacross, asks me whether I have come 'Across the word *cluideog.* It is an Easter party,' she says, and she goes on to describe it: 'We always had our cluideog in my granny's on Easter Sunday; it consisted of lighting a fire, usually in the paddock where there was a hill, boiling eggs, which my aunt had previously painted, and rolling them down, with lots of tea, with wine and maybe a drop of hard stuff for the adults.'

Your *cluideog,* Anne, comes from the Irish *clúideog, al. clúdóg,* a batch of Easter eggs. Dinneen also gives 'a small hoard', and indeed the eggs were often covered with straw and hidden all around the farm, giving the kids a great deal of fun in tracking them down. The *clúid* in your word simply means a cover or covering. I am glad that you have revived the old custom—and the word—on the Shirley estate.

Mary O'Dowd from Co. Sligo wants to know the origin of the word *helpmeet*. It came to us through a mistake. The 1611 Bible said that God created Adam's woman as 'an help meet for him'; when it was read to the masses *helpmeet* she became, and helpmeet she obstinately remained until the King's English and Dictionary surrendered and a new word was added to the language.

Really Boss, Balderdash

A teacher who is engaged in collecting Shelta words from travelling children in Co. Wexford tells me that one of their favourite expressions for something that is absolutely wonderful, is 'that's really boss'. He wants to know where the expression originated.

It seems to be slang, not Shelta: so Partridge says, at any rate. He traced it back to the United States, circa 1888; it then meant pleasant, excellent. It may have come from Dutch *baas,* master, just as boss, meaning a person in charge of others, did. It could not have come from the other *boss,* an older word now rarely used, and one which would, I fear, be considered very politically incorrect in some quarters. *Boss,* meaning a fat woman, was in vogue as far back as the 13th century. It comes from the Old French *bose,* and it originally meant a knob stud, or other circular protruberance, especially on a vault, a ceiling or a shield. Nobody told Marlowe about its political incorrectness, so that in *Tamburlaine,* Zabina, a lady 'grasse et grosse', says to Zenocrate: 'Base concubine, must thou be placed by me! That am the Empress of the mighty Turk?' Whereupon Zenocrate counters with: 'Disdainful Turkess and unreverend boss/ Call'st thou me concubine, that am bethothed/ Unto the great and mighty Tamburlaine!'

A member of Her Majesty's loyal opposition recently tried to shout down the Prime Minister at Question Time with shouts of *Balderdash!* which prompted Mrs Mary Ryan of Limerick to enquire whether the word is Irish. A very interesting word, it is a synonym for nonsense, of course, but much else besides. It is not Irish, but what its origin is is anybody's guess.

Balderdash began life as an odious concoction served in Tudor taverns. It was a mixture of small beer and buttermilk, known for its weakness; by Charles II's time the word was applied to all sorts of cocktails. In the 18th century *balderdash* was a verb as well as a noun. Smollett had some nasty things to say about the stuff sold as wine in the taverns of his day: 'A vile, unpalatable, and pernicious sophistication, balderdashed with cider, cornspirit, and the juice of sloes.'

At least it was strong, unlike the vile mixtures served in the Boar's Head in Eastcheap, where poor Jack Falstaff, playing safe by drinking sack, suspected that Mistress Quickly had balderdashed it with lime.

Flamenco, Gringo and Swift's Crux

A Kilkenny reader wants to know the origin of the word *flamenco*. She tells me that she knows me to be a fabulous dancer; obviously she doesn't know me. Has the word, she asks, anything to do with *flame*?

Divil the bit, mam, in spite of the fiery nature of the dance. The identical Spanish word simply means 'Flemish', and the dance of the Andalusian gypsies takes its name from the fact that in medieval times the Flemings had a reputation for wearing brightly coloured clothes. The lady also wants to know the origin of the word *gringo*, the nickname for foreigners in Latin America. Is it, she asks, derived from the marching song of the American soldiers, 'Green Grow the Rushes O'? Most scholars have dismissed this, and say that the word is an altered version of the Spanish *griego,* meaning 'Greek'. Presumably 'Greek' to them means or meant foreign, strange, exotic.

Finally, a reader from Dublin's Dundrum ask me to refresh his memory. He wonders if he is right in thinking that Swift coined the word *crux*, meaning a vital or decisive stage, point etc. (as in the phrase 'the crux of the matter') from Latin *crux*, cross. I am indebted to Adrian Room's excellent *Dictionary of True Etymologies* (Routledge, 1987), for the following information. The term, of course, originated as a reference to a real 'cross', with its association of torment and trouble. The usage—and the preservation of the Latin word sprang from the scholastic phrase, *crux interpretum* or *crux philosophorum*, respectively, 'torment of interpreters' or 'torment of philosophers'. Enter Swift and his friend Thomas Sheridan. From the scholastic phrases they extracted the 'crux' to mean 'riddle', 'conundrum', a linguistic entertainment (and a mental torment) they both loved. It was sometimes quite naughty. Sheridan writes: 'Dear Dean, since in cruxes and puns you and I deal,/Pray, Why is a woman a sieve and a riddle?' Swift replies: 'As for your new rebus, or riddle or crux,/I will either explain, or repay it in trucks' (odds and ends, rubbish).

I can go no further; these two prime-boys were no proponents of political correctness. Anyway, thus was 'crux' born in 1718.

Comfort and Good Cheer

Recently a good friend of mine had an unfortunate experience when out riding. He was thrown at a stone wall, landing on the only boulder in sight with his horse on top of him, and he was struck by another horse as he tried to scramble away from danger. When I enquired at the hospital I was told that I could visit him, as his condition was 'comfortable'. It was anything but, in our modern sense of the word. He had a few broken ribs and a chipped coccyx, and there he was, strung up between heaven and earth in a kind of hammock.

Comfortable indeed!

The verb *confortare* is not found in Classical Latin, I believe, but is frequently met in the Vulgate. As is evident from the *fortis* which it embodies, it means to get strong. This is the sense Wyclif had in mind when he wrote, in his translation of *Luke*, 'And the child waxed, and was counfortid.' Tyndale has 'And there appeared an angel unto Him from heaven, comforting Him.' This old meaning, used in hospital bulletins since the eight Henry's day, was the one understood by the Tudors: Shakespeare, in *As You Like It*, has 'Thy conceit is nearer death than thy powers; for my sake, be comfortable; hold death awhile at arm's end'.

Clumsy is another word whose meaning has changed utterly. It once meant 'num through cold' as John Florio's great Italian-English Dictionary put it.

Time has changed *cheer* as well. The Greeks, Cicero boasted, had no equivalent to the Latin *vultus*, the countenance. *Cheer*, in its early days, was exactly such as Cicero had in mind, 'the countenance as the ever-varying exponent of the sentiments of the soul', as one old commentator has it. So that when Wyclif wrote 'Cayn was wroot greetlie and his cheer felde down' he meant that his face fell. 'In swoot of thi cheer thou schalt ete thei breed' was his version of the well-known line from Genesis. And this is Surrey, one of the first of England's great sonneteers, circa 1540: 'Each froward threatening cheer of fortune makes us plain; And every pleasant show revives again.'

Cheers!

Rockers, Rakes and Locks

A very interesting letter arrived the other day from Zeist, from a Dutchman who, for his own reasons would like to remain anonymous. He tells me that although I was on the right track guessing that the term *racker*, an opener of gates, and a helper to those in distress during a meet of the Ward Union Hunt, might have come from the Dutch *rak*, I should have considered a more obvious Dutch word *rakker*. I would have, had I known of it! My correspondent traces the source of this word in Ireland to King Billy's day, 'a person practically unknown in my country, where his popular name means King Small Buttocks', he says. A *rakker* was a commoner who, among other things, assisted the landed gentry during hunts. Dr Brigitte van Ryckeghem of Ballinteer, in Dublin, has pointed out to me that a *rakker* was also a helper of bailiffs, a ruffian; and that racker still means a horseboy in Fingall.

Racker in parts of Wexford means (or meant—I haven't heard the term in years) a vagabond, and this work may be related to the Dutch one. However, in both Wexford and Scotland, according to the English Dialect Dictionary, a *racker* also meant a professional jester. This racker is a different word and comes from Irish *reacaire*, reciter of poems, declaimer.

Mr Brian Gaffney from Castle Avenue, Clontarf, would like to know a little about the words *rake* meaning an undefined number, or several, as in 'he drank a rake of pints', and *lock*, meaning a small quantity, as in 'bring in a lock of turf'.

Rake is defined by the English Dialect Dictionary as 'a load, as much as can be carried at one journey; a large quantity'. It is a Scots word: 'He brings two, thrie rake a day; applied to dung, coals, etc. in which carts and horses are employed. Also to the carriage of water in buckets.' It is, Wright's great dictionary says, of unknown origin.

Lock nowadays seems confined to the northern half of Ireland, but it is found all over the neighbouring island, from Scotland right down to Devon, Dorset and Cornwall. Lover had 'Cryin' a sieve full of pratees, or schreechin' a lock of savoys' in *Legends and Stories of Ireland*, back in the 1830s, when both spuds and cabbages were scarce enough items, God knows; and Thomas Hardy had 'Curl up to sleep in a lock of straw' in *Far from the Madding Crowd*, in 1874. *Lock* is Germanic in origin. Compare Low German *lok*, a number, quantity heap.

Dying Words?

A Galway reader has sent me a list of words which are according to some American computer whiz-kid, in danger of extinction. My correspondent did not mention where the newspaper cutting she sent me originated, but no matter. Many of the words listed are modern American slang words, and most of them I wouldn't shed a tear for, but to think that *crony* is on the way out is startling.

It is not of course an American word. It came into being in the days of Charles II, as did a lot of those short, useful words which had to survive the fierce onslaught of many of the great 17th and 18th-century bookmen in order to retain their place in the common man's vocabulary. *Banter* and *sham* make their appearance around 1677 and you'll find them much used in the tracts published in connection with the Popish Plot. *Whig*, then a term of abuse, came into being in connection with the promoters of the Exclusion Bill in 1679, but soon became the accepted badge of a great political party; around the same time the word *prig* was coined. *Chum* was first seen in print in 1684, *fun* in 1685, and *mob* in 1688. Swift did his best to kill these words, and railed constantly at 'the barbarity which delights in monosyllables'. He was particularly pleased to 'have done my utmost to stop the progress of *mobb* and *banter*'. Later Chesterfield and Dr Johnson took up the cudgel against *crony*. Nobody paid attention.

Crony was born in Cambridge University as student slang, and came from the Greek *khronios*, of long duration, from *khronos*, time. It is a good word, whatever old Johnson might say, suggesting a companionship used to hearing the chimes at midnight in smoky taverns. Burns knew this, and used it well when he spoke in his best poem of his hero's 'ancient, trusty, droughty crony:/Tam lo'ed him like a vera brither,/They had been fou (full) for weeks thegither.' Cronies, by the way, are exclusively male and have nothing whatever to do with crones.

Another word which appears to be dying in America is *frolic*. Originally the Dutch *vrolijk*, a 16th-century import, from Middle Dutch *vro*, happy, frolic was both English noun and adjective a century later. You will remember Milton's 'frolic wind that breathes the spring'. Herrick speaks of wine as being both 'frolic' and 'frantick'. The great university that gave us crony seems to have been a frolicsomeplace in that 17th century. That excellent gossip, Thomas Woodcock, wrote of Dr Thomas Goodwin, an esteemed Fellow, no less: 'He was somewhat whimsycall, and in a frolick pist once in old Mr Lothian's pocket. This I suppose was before his trouble of conscience made him serious.'

Oh, happy days!

More Birds

Mrs J. O'Sullivan, who lives near Tipperary town, asks whether anybody now uses the lovely collective nouns one found in the schoolbooks of her youth, such as a *charm* of birds, an *exhaltation* of larks. I hope so, dear reader, but I very much doubt it.

An *exhaltation* of larks (from Latin *exaltare*, to raise, from *altus*, high) is at least as old as Herrick, and as for the equally delightful *charm* of birds, particularly finches, although the word is certainly related to that which means the quality of pleasing people, I think that we should look elsewhere to find the connection with birds. Collins suggests that *charm*, meaning a flock of birds, may be a S.W. England dialect word, related to *chirm*, a loud noise as of a number of people chattering or of birds singing. Perhaps, but I prefer to think of a charm of birds as coming from Old French *charme*, from the Latin *carmen*, song, from *cantare*, to sing. Surely singing was what Milton had in mind when he wrote in *Paradise Lost*: 'Sweet is the breath of morn,/Her rising sweet,/With charm of earliest birds.'

May I here give greeting from Spain to Ireland's most distinguished birdman, Major Robin Ruttledge, of Newcastle, Co. Wicklow, from a mutual friend, Ian Gibson, Lorca's distinguished biographer, who as a Trinity student in the 50s learned all his bird lore from the master in the fields between Newcastle and the sea.

A reader who lives in Mooncoin, Co. Kilkenny, wants to know the origin of the word *ragamuffin*, a ragged, unkempt child. The original *Ragamoffyn* was a fiend, mentioned in *Piers Plowman* in 1393. There seems to be no mention of this little divil prior to that date, which has led most commentators to suggest that Langland invented the name. The first element in the word suggests rag, of course, and *ffyn* reminds us of fiend, but let's not get carried away—there may be no connection.

Another word for a ragamuffin is *tatterdemalion,* a word now on the brink of extinction, according to some dictionaries. The first element of this good word, first seen in print in the 17th century is self-evident; many dictionaries cite the Old French *maillon*, swaddling clothes, as a basis for the second. I'm not so sure. Perhaps they should consider the Italian *maglia*, shirt of mail, later undershirt. I think a tattered vest makes better sense in this case than a tattered nappy.

Barmy

Mr John Hennessy, who works in Kilburn, London, wants to know what the origin of the word *barmy* is. He is intrigued by an explanation he read recently, one which does not agree with those given in the major dictionaries. This is the gist of what he read:

When Henry VIII suppressed the monasteries some of the church properties were spared and converted to other uses. The Hospice of St Mary Bethlehem was converted to an asylum for the insane. The wards of Bethlehem, pronounced Bedlam by the populace, were named after various saints. One of these was St Bartholomew's, and the non-violent inmates of this ward were often allowed out to beg on the streets. The Londoners of old Henry's time must have been fierce bad at the pronunciation: they made St Barmy of St Bartholomew, 'through the same process of slurring that made Bedlam of Bethlehem', according to Mr Hennessy's source.

I doubt that, somehow. I prefer the authorised version which says that *barmy* comes from *barm*, first seen in print in the 16th century. *Barm* was the yeasty froth on fermenting malt liquors. It was also an archaic or dialect word for yeast. *Barm* comes from Old English *bearm*, related to *beran*, to bear, Old Norse *barmr*, barm. The connection between a furiously bubbling froth and madness is, I think, pretty obvious.

In rural Lancashire they still make *barm-cakes*, round flat soft bread rolls. These are not *barm-bracks,* loaves with currants in them (from Irish *báirín breac*, speckled loaf). I remember being corrected in primary school for not spelling the word *barm-brack*.

This whole barmy business brings me to a very interesting letter from a Dublin lady who came to us by the grace of Cupid from Norfolk. She tells me that in her youth the local phrase for not being quite the full shilling was 'He gets no further than Wednesday'. I found the phrase in Wright's *English Dialect Dictionary* (1905); but above it was a more interesting one. What was it about the word Wednesday that made the English and Scots invoke it as a charm against goblins, witches, warlocks and all things that go bump in the night?

There is a phrase found in both Norfolk and parts of southern Scotland: '*It's Wednesday through all the world*'; and if you say this it will banish evil. My correspondent says that her grandmother used to end the night prayers with the phrase. Ireland, it seems, is not the only place where the old pishogues remain.

Liverpool English

Mrs June Wheatley tells me that she is a Dublin woman who has been living in Liverpool for many years. It is apparent from her letter that she has, as they say, a great ear for the often stigmatised working-class speech of her adopted city, an accent combining features of Lancashire, Irish and, to a lesser extent, Welsh English introduced by 19th- and 20th-century immigrants, many of them seafaring people and their families. (The word *Scouse* comes from the 18th century *lobscouse*, a sailor's stew of meat, ship's biscuits and vegetables; a sailor was known as a *lobscouser*.)

The admirable *Oxford Companion to the English Language*, edited by Tom McArthur, a 1,184-page hardback bargain at £25, has an informative page on Liverpool English, but it could teach Mrs Wheatley very little. As evidence of the Irish connection they both point out the Dublin and Liverpool tendency to replace a /t/ between vowels by an /r/, often showed in print by rr, which gives us the Dub's *exirra* and *delirra*, and the Scouse's *what's the marra?* Working-class Liverpool Catholics say *dese tree* for *these three*, and *muntth* for *month*; McArthur points out that until recently it was possible to distinguish the speech of Irish Catholic Scousers from Protestant English through the pronunciation of some words; a double advertisement on local buses in the 1960s read on one side of the bus, *Treat us furly, travel early*, on the other *Treat us fairly, travel airly* (the latter denoting Irish-derived usage).

Mrs Wheatley refers to what is, perhaps, the most interesting feature of Scouse, the adenoidal quality that pervades it. She finds it irritating and wonders what gave rise to it. The great phonetician David Abercrombie, was the first to notice that children often imitate other kids who have speech defects, and he went on: 'A striking example is afforded by some urban slum communities where adenoids, due doubtless to malnutrition and lack of sunlight, are prevalent, with their consequent effect on voice quality, but where people can be found with adenoidal voice quality who do not have adenoids—they have learned the quality from the large number who do have them, so that they conform to what, for that community, has become the norm. The accent of Liverpool seems to have had its origins in such circumstances.'

McArthur quotes both Abercrombie and Gerald Knowles's essay on the controversial adenoidal factor in Trudgill (ed.) *Sociolinguistic Patterns in British English* (1978).

He also quotes me three times in his book, but don't let that deter you from buying it.

Box-fast and Sleaving Ropes

A man who trains slow racehorses in the north of England recently explained on a television programme that two of his horses were *box-fast* with a virus. He had to explain the term to his interviewer. In the south of England, as in Ireland, most of the words ending in *fast*, meaning *fixed*, have had their day and are no longer in use. *Steadfast* survives everywhere, and if *box-fast*, meaning confined to his box or stable, survives, perhaps so does *bed-fast*, common in New Ross in my grandmother's time and recorded in Antrim by G.B. Adams about 30 years ago.

Shame-fast was altered by a spelling mistake to *shamefaced*. Old Chaucer had it right when he spoke of '*shame-fast chastitee*', which you and I might gloss as chastity firmly rooted in modesty; but Kyd, Shakespeare and Marlowe had *shame-fac'd*, and the error survived. Perhaps we should be grateful. Shame-faced is a more striking epithet than shamefast, I think.

You'll find *shaamfast* in Poole's *Glossary of the Dialect of Forth and Bargy*, compiled at the end of the 18th century, and I recorded the word in Carne in 1978 from 90-year-old Phil Wall.

Sleaving ropes aboard ships in hard weather was painful work, he told me, and caused rheumatism. Here was the word John Donne used in his invitation to the river. To *sleave,* from Old English *slæfan,* is to disentangle, to tease out: in Wall's, case, a rope into its component strands, in Donne's, a lure of silken floss from thicker silk: 'Let coarse bold hands, from slimy nest/The bedded fish in banks out-wrest,/Let curious traitors sleave silke flies/To witch poore wandring fishes' eyes.'

Shakespeare, as every Leaving Cert student knows, or should know, used sleave as a noun, although many of them, I suppose, think that Macbeth's 'ravelled (Middle Dutch *ravellen)* sleave' (of care) means a frayed or tangled sleeve. But *sleave* has nothing to do with *sleeve* and Shakespeare's ravelled sleave is ragged, unstitched silk.

H.C. Hart

H.C. Hart (1847) is one of the unsung heroes of Irish lexicography. He was educated at Portora and at Trinity, was a botanist of repute and went with Admiral Markham to the North Pole in 1875–6, and to Sinai and Arabia with Kitchener and Hull in 1884. He wrote books on the flora of these regions, as well as works on the flora of Aran (1875), Mayo and Galway (1883), Howth (1887) and Donegal (1898). He lectured at the Queen's College, Galway and in 1895 became High Sheriff of his beloved Donegal.

He began his collection of dialect words about 1880 and published a paper on Donegal English in 1899. He did not live to see his glossary in print, but Michael Traynor incorporated it in his *The English Dialect of Donegal,* published by the Royal Irish Academy in 1957. Most of his words are still in common use, I'm happy to say, because the people of the northern counties treasure their distinctive speech.

Aboon, also found as *abeen,* is common in the mountainous region between Churchill and Gweedore. Both words mean above, or beyond. *Up aboon* means upstairs. Hart heard, '*He came from abeen Churchill.*'

The botanist's glossary does, of course, contain many of the local words for wildflowers and grasses. *Pretty Betsy* is the red valerian; *farrabun* was applied to various flowers of Order Ranunculaceae, such as the buttercup and the crowfoot (Dinneen has *fearbán,* the creeping crowfoot); *barradu* he glosses as 'a fibrous cluster of roots of bent or some other sand plant which is used in scouring pans, etc. in Fanad'. It comes from the Irish *barrach duimhche, barrach,* tow + *duimhche,* gen. of *dumhach,* a dune. *Srouch* is a lovely word. (Pronounce the *ch* as you would the *ch* in loch.) It means the sigh of wind or the murmur of the sea or a river.

In Glenalla Hart heard the word *cooshee*. It means the prance of a horse. 'He gave a cooshee here and a cooshee there till he brasted the harness'. Perhaps the horse got too much *hannels*, which meant food, drink and care. *Gosther* means to chatter, to waste time talking; hence *gostherin'*, gossiping, idling, wasting time.

These words, and hundreds of others, are still to be heard in the *loaning* (boreens) of Donegal where Hart heard them a hundred years ago. Michael Traynor's book is out of print, more's the pity. It merits a second edition.

Partridge

The poet Cowper summed us up pretty well: 'Philologists who chase/A panting syllable through time and space/Start it at home, and hunt it in the dark,/To Gaul, to Greece and into Noah's Ark.'

A stimulating chase it can often be and, for my part, I prefer the hunters who give us a plausible etymology to those who play safe and tell us that the origin of a word is obscure, and leave it at that.

The late Eric Honeywood Partridge was a bold and brilliant scholar. He never got the recognition that far lesser men got, mainly, I suspect, because of a deep suspicion of his astounding learning harboured by some of his university counterparts. He seemed to understand this, though he held no grudges. 'The trouble,' he once said, 'is that some people shrink from marching to the horizon, for fear (an early medieval fear) of falling over the world's edge.'

The slang word *phoney* was practically unknown outside North America before 1939, when journalists in the likes of *Life* and *Time* magazines began to tell us on this side of the world about 'the phoney war'. The word gained currency and it is still widely used. Some suggested that the phrase *'funny business'* was the origin the word; others thought that it came from (tele)*phone*. Others still thought that a man called *Forney*, a jeweller who specialised in imitations, gave us the word.

Partridge solved the problem to my satisfaction at least. In *Origins* (1990 ed., Routledge, £49.50) he suggested that the word came to us via American *phoney man*, a peddler of imitation jewellery, from its original, the English *fawney man,* itself an adaptation of the British *fawney cove*, one who practices the the *fawney rig*, or ringdropping trick, involving a gilt ring passed off as gold. This trick, Partridge says, was first described by George Parker in *A View of Society*, first published in 1781. The key word is the underworld *fawney*, a finger-ring; none other than our Irish word *fáinne,* brought to England, no doubt, by Irish confidence tricksters. From there it travelled on the emigrant ships to America.

Homer in Scots

In 1940 the Saltire Society published the *Selected Poems* of James Hogg as the first of a Scottish Classic series which continued intermittently until 1959, when the society published *Gavin Douglas. A Selection of His Poetry*. Douglas translated the complete *Aeneid* into Scots; and now the Saltire Society have given, us in a beautiful paperback which contains superb prints by Barbara Robertson, *Tales Frae The Odyssey O Homer Owreset Intil Scots* by William Neill. I had previously read him in English and Gaelic; he has now made claim to his full inheritance as a Scots man-of-letters.

Of the three languages he writes so well in, Neill says that 'Scots alane bides a puir orphant, for aa that maist fowk in Scotland ken it in some meisure. Lik Gaelic, it wes the speik o palace, coort an college at yae (one) time. Nou it is lukkt doun on bi cockapenties ettlin (attempting) taw yird (bury) it lang afore its daith.'

But is Scots a living tongue? Is writing in Scots not mere dictionary-dredging? Was it not dying in the time of Robert Burns? No, replies Neill. 'It was gey (good) an vieve (lively) whan I wes a bit laddie in Ayrshire an tis no deid nou tae onybody wi lugs tae hear. Gin (if) ye can read this, Scots isna deid, an I'm gey (good) and shair (sure) thare's monie a body wha reads this buik will hear the wards soondin in their heids.'

They are still soondin in mine. A taoscán to whet your appetite:

Sae spak he; straucht (*straight away*) the watter steyed, the swaw (*wave*) held back, an the river lown (*calm*) afore brocht him til the firth an he lat his knees gie wey an drappt his michtie nieves (*mighty fists*) for his hairt wes sair (*sore*) caa'd (*knocked*) doun bi the sea. An his flesh wes aa swait up an the saut (*salt*) watter rinnin wi a scoosh oot frae his mooth an his neb. (*nose*). Thare athoot (*without*) speik or braith (*breath*) he wes fair forfochen (*exhausted*) an a muckle weariness cam ower him.

This treasure of a book, which contains a glossary, can be bought from The Saltire Society, 9 Fountain Close, 22 High Street, Edinburgh EH1 1TF. An audio cassette recording of parts of it is also available.

Pet

The Irish word *peata*, I was once told in school, is a borrowing from English, its origin being *pet*. The reverse is true.

In the Royal Irish Academy's *Contributions to a Dictionary of the Irish Language* (fasciculus ed. Maud Joynt) we find *pet(t)a,* masculine, nom. pl. *pet(t)ai* and *petada,* according to Vendryes in *Revue Celtique,* XLIV, 308ff., a word of native origin meaning a pet, usually of a tame or domesticated animal: '*indat pettai sút no indat éoin chena?* (= are those tame or wild birds?). We also find the word in the ancient Laws of Ireland, in *Félire Oengusso,* which dates from the early ninth century; and the word is to be found also in the early 16th-century *Book of Lismore*. The twelfth-century *Cath Catharda,* the Irish version of Lucan's, *Pharsalia,* has the word *pet(t)acht,* taming, domesticating. Of persons, Dáibhí O Bruadair, (died circa 1689), has *peata* meaning a fop, or milksop.

I should mention that Stokes, in his *Linguistic Value of the Irish Annals* wrote that *pet(t)a* came from some French cognate of *petit*; I believe that his suggestion is not accepted nowadays.

I am told that the lovely English word, *pet,* when used as a term of endearment, has recently been added to the list banished from their lexicon by the English departments of two minor mid-western American universities. The word is politically incorrect, according to the prairie scholars. When will this nonsense stop?

Peata, by the way, is still used as a term of endearment in Irish. It is still politically correct to call your loved one *peata ceana* (gen. of *cion,* love, affection). Gaeltacht people, I fear, wouldn't feel at home on the range.

Gigs and Jigs

A Co. Monaghan reader writes to ask about the origin of the word *gig,* meaning a single booking for musicians.

Neither the Oxford nor the Collins dictionaries can offer any satisfactory theory as to the word's provenance, but the conjecture of C.R. Baskervill in his masterly study, *The Elizabethan Jig,* is that the word *gig* is a doublet of *jig:* two words with a common onomatopoeic source now forgotten, but undoubtedly one with sexual connotations. (He reminds us of the large number of vulgar puns on both words in Renaissance literature.)

Baskervill discarded one of Oxford's theories that *gig* and its doublet, *jig* are related to the obsolete French *gigeur,* to leap or frolic, on the grounds that there is no convincing link between them, except, perhaps, a parallel onomatopoeic influence.

Jeffrey Pulver, the musicologist, also regards *jig* as a doublet of *gig,* meaning anything round , or revolving, which he derives from the Icelandic *geiga:* Certainly the ordinary Elizabethan meaning of *gig* is a child's top. Though we know little of the medieval and renaissance jig as dance there are references to the jig dancer's 'turning like a top', 'dancing like a whirlygig, and 'wheeling until giddy'.

As to whether the jig was primarily a dance, distinct in kind and musical form, or whether it derived from the dance-ballad is a matter scholars still argue about. But in Shakespeare's time a combination of song and dance, called both *jig* and *gig* (in various spellings) was still a living creative force, performed after the Epilogue for the delectation of the groundings; a song-and-dance routine often condemned by the Puritans for 'their mimicke venerean action', as the anonymous author of one tract on the 'lasciuious Gigge' put it.

So at one time or another both *gig* and *jig* meant a dance, a ballad-dance, a country song with dancing (Florio in his *World of Words,* 1518, defines *strambotti* as 'countrie gigges' and *chiarantana* as a 'kind of Caroll or song full of leaping like a Scottish gigge'), a duet with dancing between the verses, a bawdy song-and-dance playlet, and 'the music of the voice for dancing' (George Gascoigne, 1576).

That latter definition might well be remembered by Comhaltas Ceoltóirí Eireann, which has discarded the good old word *jigging* for *lilting.* Not in deference to any surviving Puritan mores I trust.

Shall and Will

A Co. Cork teacher has a problem with the Irish usage *of shall* and *will*. No matter how many times she explains the matter, her pupils use will in every instance in their essays. She wants to know why we Irish confuse these words.

Grammarians have always thought it their business to prescribe and to proscribe in matters of language use. It is, of course, none of their business to do so, but they are responsible for the confusion regarding *will* and *shall*. The Tudor writers had no difficulty at all with the two words: they simply didn't recognise any distinction between them. Neither did any grammar published before 1622. Along came John Wallis in 1653, and in his *Grammatica Linguae Anglicanae* he prescribed for the benefit of foreigners, the Irish included, that simple futurity should be expressed by *shall* in the first person, and by *will* in the second and third. In 1755 Dr Johnson took it upon himself in his Dictionary to prescribe the rule governing questions, and ten years later William Ward in his *Grammar of the English Language* laid down the full set of laws which, he hoped, would henceforth govern all writers of English. Nobody paid much notice to Mr Ward until 1795 when Lindley Murray wrote a grammar which echoed his prescriptions, a book widely used by successive generations of teachers. The distinction between *shall* and *will* was not, however, observed in colloquial speech, as the language of the English and Irish stageshows; and it is today commonly ignored except by speakers who consciously conform to the Ward/Murray rules or, as in the case of the Cork children, are recipients of a tradition which has not been influenced by these rules.

The late Professor Alan Bliss, a Londoner, once said that Irish people should write *will* in every case; he could not see why we should ape the English of our neighbours. He pointed out that the craze for standardisation was born in an age that greatly feared language change. Hadn't Bacon, at the end of his days, fearing that the ever-changing English would 'play the bankrupts' with his books, had them translated into Latin?

What our Department of Education inspectors would say to Bliss I have no idea, Mrs Walsh. Why don't you ask them? I, for one, would love to know what they think.

A recent letter to the editor accuses me of inaccurate and misleading statements regarding *shall* and *will*. J.A. Richmond cites Mulloy's *The Irish Difficulty* (1887). This book is one of a 19th-century group which, 'on the basis of assumed distinctions of meaning, attempt to give rules and principles for the *correct* use of *shall* and *will*. These rules range in number, completeness, and simplicity, from a single sentence to the 47 pages of refinements and explanations found in Mulloy's book. Not only are these rules, after being laid down, used to interpret special instances with meanings that fit the rule, but where such interpretation is absolutely impossible the usage is condemned as wrong.'

I quote from the most important study of *shall* and *will* in Modern English, that of Charles Fries in *PMLA* XL, 1925. J.R. Hulbert in *PMLA* 62, 1947, and Albert Baugh in *The History of the English Language* (1935) confirm that the Tudors made no consistent distinction between the two words. For every time that Shakespeare and Queen Bess herself in her letters, conform to what the 18th- and 19th-century grammarians prescribed as correct, Hulbert and Fries can give us many more instances of 'mistakes' made by them.

This is Fries in his *American English Grammar* (New York, 1940): 'The conventional rules for *shall* and *will* did not arise from any attempt to describe the practice of the language as it actually was either before the 18th century or at the time the grammar was written in which these rules first appeared. The authors of these grammars, Lowth (1762) and Ward (1765), definitely repudiated usage . . . That the general usage of *shall* and *will* did not at any time during the history of Modern English agree with the conventional rules is a conclusion that can be reasonable drawn . . .'

The intellectual temper of the 18th century led to a concern for stability, for a grammar based on Reason, but the grammarians' squabbles led only to utter confusion. (Hazlitt in his grammar of 1810 went further than Ward's distinction by declaring that we cannot *under any circumstances* ask a question with *will* in the first person.) As for the reduced form, always atonic and written as 'll (as in *I'll* or *we'll*), practically all who have written on this subject interpret it as being a contraction for *will* only.

Finally, an examination of the newspapers of England will convince anybody of the silliness of Mulloy's theory that in England the proper use of shall and will '. . . is acquired by a sort of natural instinct'.

Kitty, Glar, Glit, Dailigone

A lady with an address in London wrote to ask about the provenance of the word *kitty,* the pool of money in card games. All the great dictionaries give it as of uncertain origin, but I think it may have come from the common dialect word *kit,* a wooden tub used by housewives for storing odds and ends. (Hence, by the way, *kit* meaning personal equipment.) We have the Middle English *kitt,* and its variant *kytt;* Middle Dutch *kitte* and *kit,* and the Dutch *kit,* a jug. But let's leave the last word to Partridge (*Origins,* Routledge, 1990). Having agreed that the origin of *kitty* is uncertain, and that it may, indeed, be connected with *kit,* a tub, he goes on to quote the ingenious musings of a friend: '*kitty, kitty,* diminutive of *Kate* (pet-form of *Catharine/Catherine*) erudite pun on French *quête,* as in *faire la quête,* to take up the collection in

church: Old French–Middle French *queste*, seeking, compare English *quest*.
Compare, semantically, the approximately synonymous French slang, *la
cathérine*.' Full marks for inventiveness, at any rate.

A man from Sion Mills, Co. Tyrone, wants to know where the word
bottle, so commonly used nowadays by soccer commentators, comes from.
Paul Beale, editor of Partridge's *Concise Dictionary of Slang*, says that it is 20th-
century rhyming slang: *bottle and glass=arse, though* I am at a loss to understand
why the loss of a footballer's fundament could be equated with timidity or
worse.

A Westmeath reader is stymied by some dialect words italicised in Séamus
Heaney's poem, 'Fostering' (*Seeing Things*, 1991): 'I can't remember never
having known/ The immanent hydraulics of a land/ Of *glar* and *glit* and
floods at *dailigone*.'

Glar is soft, liquid mud, Irish *glár*; *glit* is ooze or slime, especially green
slime on water. *Glet is* more common in Donegal and Scotland; and as for
dailigone, I am most reliably informed that this lovely word is a form of *daylight
gone*: dusk, twilight, nightfall. It is to be found, too, hidden under the
head-word *day*, in Traynor's *English Dialect of Donegal*.

Pleach and Plash, Sally and Willow

A few weeks ago near the estuary of the lordly Barrow I saw a man mending
lobster pots by plaiting sally rods. He was *pleaching* them, he told me; he
pronounced the word *playchin*. *Pleaching* has been around for quite a while.
In the 14th century we find *plechen*, from Old North French *plechier*, from
Latin *plectere*, to weave, plait. I had heard the word only once previously,
used by the chanteuse of Neamstown, Co. Wexford, the late Liz Jeffries. Mrs
Jeffries, describing one of the local beauties, said that the young lady in
question was a bit old for pleaching her hair.

There is another word, *plash*, which is related to *pleach*. Collins says that
it is from Old French *plassier*, from *plais*, hedge, woven fence, and, like *pleach*,
from Latin *plectere*. Is it used in Ireland, I wonder?

These lovely words deserve to live. 'Shaksper, the Stratford clown', as
somebody was pleased to call him, knew *pleach*. Antony says to his page,
Eros, when their world had turned upside down:

Would'st thou be window'd in great Rome and see
Thy master thus with pleach'd arms, bending down
His corrigible neck, his face subdued
To penetrative shame . . .

Tennyson and Swinburne in their dreams of fair ladies spoke of the
pleaching of blonde hair. They would have been at home in Neamstown,

in the heart of the Norman/Flemish country of Forth and Bargy, where you can still find young women who seem to have walked straight out of a Vermeer.

Sally, I was assured by the American author of a recent essay on Yeats, is 'a Hiberno-English word, unknown in England'. It is no such thing. *The English Dialect Dictionary* recorded it in almost every county in England. I find it strange that Collins omits it, probably relegating it to dialect status, while the English Dialect Dictionary has no record of its sister, the mournfully beautiful *sallow*. (Old English *sealh,* Old Norse *selja,* Latin *salix).*

Keats has:

Then in a wailful choir the small gnats mourn
Among the river sallows.

And Hopkins asks us to

Look, look! A May-mess, like on orchard boughs.
Look! March-blooms, like meal'd-with-yellow sallows.

They are all *willows*, of course, to my mind the most beautiful word of the three. It comes from O.E. *welig*, related to *wilige*, the medieval word for what the man by the Barrow was mending—a wicker basket.

Influence

A recent discussion on the merits and demerits of various vaccines in a medical journal left—inadvertently, I hope—among the glossy magazines in a doctor's waiting room, remind me of the provenance of the word *influenza* and of various cognate words.

Influenza is Italian, of course, a learned borrowing from Medieval Latin *influentia*, itself derived originally from Latin *influere*, to flow in. *Influere* has present participle *influens*, whence Old French *influence*, whence English *influence*, defined in the days of old as the power of the stars over the characters and destinies of men and considered to be an ethereal fluid streaming towards earth from the stars.

In John Milton's *Nativity Hymn*: 'The Stars with deep amaze/Stand fixt with stedfast gaze/Bending one way their precious influence.'

The translators of the Bible had previously asked the question, 'Canst thou bind the sweet influences of the Pleiades?'; Shakespeare, too, was very much aware of the celestial inflow. Prospero had his eye on 'A most auspicious star, whose influence,/If now I court not, but omit, my fortune/Will ever after droop'.

The inspirational influence of beautiful women was acknowledged even by Milton, whose personal experience of the species was not a happy one, so that we hear the great poet speak of 'Ladies whose bright eyes/ Rain influence.'

Crashaw speaks of a cherub who sips 'sweet influence' from a woman's eyes and 'so adds sweetness to his sweetest lips'.

Dear me, look what has happened to this lovely word.

The magic has gone and we have baneful as well as beneficial influence; and worse still we have that acute, infectious viral respiratory disease that killed 20 million people in the aftermath of the Great War. Milton! thou should'st be living at this hour.

Dusk

A man from Derry, who first reminded me of Seamus Heaney's *dailigone,* that lovely word for nightfall, tells me that the people of his part of the world have other words for that time of evening: *day-light-falling, day-fall, dellit-fall, duskies* and *duskiss.* I've heard *duskling* in Co. Wexford, and the English Dialect Dictionary has *doosling,* a variant from Lincolnshire. In the farmhouses around Cheltenham you'll hear the word *dimpsy* used for twilight.

All these words, and let us include *dusk* and *twilight* for good measure, are so sweet-sounding that Milton seems to hit a strange note when he says, 'As when the Sun. . . . In dim Eclips *disastrous twilight* sheds'. Shakespeare, too, spoke of 'Disasters in the sun', but disaster originally meant something wrong with the stars and so an ill-starred occurrence.

The lovely *dusk* came on the heels of the adjective *dusky.* Shakespeare would not have understood what we mean by dusk, although he might have called it the dusky hour. Incidentally, he wouldn't have used twilight either. Dusk comes from Old English, *dox,* related to Old Saxon *dosan,* brown, Norwegian *dusmen,* misty, all from Latin *fuscus,* dark brown.

To dusk, meaning to make dark, is as old as Chaucer. Housman used the verb intransitively: 'I see the air benighted/And all the duskling dales,/And lamps in England lighted/And evening wrecked in Wales.'

A word whose meaning changed considerably in the last century is the beautiful *darkling,* which for some reason came to be regarded as the participle of 'to darkle'. A natural enough error, claims the Scottish word-man, Ivor Brown: if day sparkled, why should not night darkle? But when Keats wrote 'Darkling I listen' in his *Ode to a Nightingale* he didn't mean that he was going black in the face, merely that he was standing in the dark. Moore, on the other hand, wrote 'when matter darkles or when spirit beams'. Keats, unlike Moore and Byron, was following the old masters: 'Out went the candle and we were left darkling', says the Fool in *Lear.*

Darkle, like *sidle,* is a back-formation. *Sidle* is back-formed from *side-ling* or *side-long,* Ivor Brown couldn't resist the quip that while W. Shakespeare and C. Marlowe went side-ling home after a night on the tiles, Tom Moore and Byron sidled, as the nights darkled.

Crack

The constant Gaelicisation of the good old English/Scottish dialect word crack as *craic* sets my teeth on edge. It seems, indeed, that many people think that the word is an Irish one; hence we find advertisements proclaiming 'music, songs, dancing and craic'; the implication is that *craic* = boozing and high jinks, great fun as it used to be, an tan do bhíodar Gaeil in Éirinn beo.

The *English Dialect Dictionary* (Wright's) deals at length with *crack,* a word still in use from the English midlands to Glasgow and Edinburgh. It gives crack as '1. talk, conversation, gossip, chat'. In this context Scott uses it in Rob Roy (1817), 'I maun hai a crack wil an auld acquaintance here'. 'The friendly crack, the cheerfulsang', wrote a lesser Caledonian, Picken, in 1813. 2. A tale, a good story or joke; gossip, scandal. 'A' cracks are not tae be trow'd', is a Scots proverb. 'Tell your crack/Before them a', wrote Burns in *The Authors Cry,* in 1786. 'To ca' the crack', in Yorkshire, means to keep the conversation going. The Irish crack, with its connotations of ribaldry and divilment in general, came to us, I suppose, by way of Donegal emigrants, who have borrowed many good words from their Scottish friends.

May I be forgiven for telling you that until this age of ecumenism the ministers of the Presbyterian church were known in the Rosses as the *friskum-tearums.* I have no idea what the provenance of that is, but I am assured that it came originally from Scotland. Of course, words such as that would be used only by *ceo-boys* or *teoboys* (ruffians, provenance unknown); or by *snugadauns* (see Dinneen *snag, snagaire,* a sneak), or by *lahoaches,* big, ignorant people, provenance unknown to me) or by *snippadauns* (cute hoors, provenance unknown, as well). I must snoak out a few more Northern words for future columns. *Snoak* is a good Donegal/Scottish word that probably came from Swedish *snoka,* to search after, or for, something. Small world!

More Crack

Mr Brendan Ellis, in a letter to the Editor of the *Irish Times,* asks if I would consider the Irish *creach,* booty, plunder, as the origin of *crack,* and the hideous (in my view) neologism, *craic.* No, I wouldn't, I'm afraid.

The Anglo-Irish (I use the term in its linguistic sense) *crack* is a recent offspring of the English/Scottish dialect word, which, for hundreds of years, has, as I pointed out, meant talking, gossiping, shooting the breeze, as the Americans say. My friend, Nora Patrick O'Donnell from Dún Lúiche in the

Donegal Gaeltacht, assures me that it was in this sense that *crack* was used in Irish conversation in her youth. The world as defined by Collins as fun, informal entertainment, is of very recent origin. Beale, in *A Concise Dictionary of Slang,* says that dates from circa 1976, but I am willing to concede that it is somewhat older than that. How then did it develop? I am convinced that the Irish labourers simply rose the acceptance level of their neighhours' *crack* to 90 on whatever metaphysical scale they use to measure these matters; the very recent birth of the Anglo-Irish *crack* would, in my view, make Mr Ellis's theory untenable, even if one could make his leap of faith in connecting a word for plunder with a word for fun.

Where then does the word *crack* in all its forms, come from? I believe that it is echoic, and that it reached us from the Middle English, *cracken, craken,* which meant to boast as well as to break, crash or crack, from the Old English *cracian,* related to Old High German *krahhon,* and, *siar amach,* to the Sanskrit *gárjati,* he shouts, roars.

Miss Jennifer Blount of Cork wants to know what the origin of acronyms such as SWALK (sealed with a loving kiss), sometimes found on the backs of teenagers' letters is. I've heard that the lovers' acronyms, at least, were first used by British servicemen as code words during the Great War: an indication of the soldier's location if this were secret. Of course boarding school wide-boys got in on the act; many of my generation will have seen things like SWALCAKWS (sealed with a lick 'cause a kiss won't stick) on the back of love letters. I'm sure, too, that many's the Reverend Mother wondered what acronyms such as LYKAH, popular among *the gorseyjacks* (Wexford word, origin unknown to me) of my day, meant. The estimable Beale had to consult his uncle Max about it. It meant, of course, leave your knickers at home. The cad!

The Twangman

A lady from Balbriggan who is an admirer of the Dublin ballad singer, Frank Harte, wrote to ask some interesting questions about words found in the old Dublin song *The Twangman.*

She has, by the way, an interesting theory about the origin of the word *cant,* defined by Collins as 'specialised vocabulary of a particular group, such as thieves, journalists or lawyers'. It was, says Collins, probably introduced via Norman French *canter,* to sing, from Latin *cantare;* and was used disparagingly, from the twelfth century, of chanting in religious services. But could it not, asks my correspondent, have been introduced directly from the Irish *caint*? Indeed it could. As early as 1567 we find 'to cant' glossed as 'to speak' in Thomas Harman's *A Caveat or Warening for common cursetors* (disbarred lawyers, ex Latin *currere,* to run).

Pé scéal é, what, my correspondent asks, is a *twangman*, of whom Mr Harte sings so well in his definitive recording? Well, the *twangman* was the male participant in a notorious double act called *buttock and twang*. The *buttock* was a prostitute, who was followed at a distance in her nocturnal ramblings by her *twang*. A tract called *Highwaymen*, written by Alexander Smith in 1714, and quoted by Partridge in his *Dictionary of the Underworld*, gives us further information. 'She went upon the Buttock and Twang by Night, which is picking up a Cull, Cully or Spark, and pretending not to expose her face in a Publick House, she takes him into some dark Alley, so while the decoy'd Fool is groping her with his Breeches down, she picks his Fob or Pocket, of his Watch or Money, and giving a sort of Hem as a signal she hath succeeded in her Design, and then the Fellowe with whom she keeps Company, blundering up in the dark, he knocks down the Gallant, and carries off the Prize!'

Twang is of uncertain origin, but is probably echoic; it was a cant word in Beaumont and Fletcher's time, and was first glossed by them in *The Beggar's Bush* in 1615. It means what you think it might mean.

Poppets and Moppets

There was a time when the words *poppet*, *moppet* and *minikin* came amusingly and agreeably to the female ear. *Poppet* is a corruption of puppet, and because today's young woman would bridle at being thought of as anybody's plaything, the old word must soon fall into disuse and be lost forever, just like *minikin*, which is a pretty word for anything small and nice. The word comes from the Dutch *minneken*, diminutive of *minne*, love; and it died out in most places because of the confusion with *manikin*, from Dutch *manniken*, diminutive of *man*, which started life as a word for a dwarf and ended up in the medical schools of the 18th century as one for the anatomical model of a fully developed foetus.

Moppet lived for a long time, and it now seems very strange indeed that women once liked it. For *moppet* is an affectionate form of *mop* or *moppe*, which was applied as a termination to the name of fish. So that a *cod-mop* was a codling, a *herring-mop* was the young one of that species. Who now would call his beloved his sardine or his trout? Yet such was the old way. 'I called her Moppe, wrote the worthy Puttenham in *English Poesie*, 'understanding by this word a little pretty lady or tender young thing, for so we call fishes'. How we arrived at mop, young fish, from mop, rag doll, nobody knows.

The women of the Tudor stage used some lovely words of endearment. Take Ben Jonson's gentle *moonling;* which meant a nice man, but slightly feckless, a dreamer of dreams. I like most words that end in *ling* (Old English, of Germanic origin). My Wexford grandmothers *kitling* comes to mind. Herrick has *younglings*. He asks the primroses to tell him why there are dewy tears in their hearts: 'Speak whim'pring Younglings and make known/The Reason why/Ye droop and weep./Is it for want of sleep?/Or Childish Lullaby?' Tudor children played with kitlings. Herrick, like my granny, preferred them to kittens, and so do I: 'Yet can thy humble roof maintain a choir/Of singing crickets by the fire,/And the brisk mouse may feed her self with crumbs/Till that the green-eyed kitling comes.'

Kitling lives on in rural England. It's a long time since I heard it in Ireland. A letter from Máire Nic Mhaoláin, of Dalkey, delighted me. My grandmother's word *kittling* for kitten was, she tells me, in use in east Co. Down in her youth. Indeed it seems to have been used all over Ulster, as well as in Scotland and in northern and midland England. 'That other night ye boiled the drownded kittlin' in me stirabout', complained a character in *Maguire,* a story by Seumus MacManus. Burns has the phrase 'as cantie as a kittlin' in *Halloween* (1785). Cantie means brisk, lively. My correspondent also informs me that even more common in east Down was the verb, *kittle,* e.g. the cat kittled.

My thanks, too, to Leslie Matson of Cork and to John Cameron of Dún Laoghaire for pointing out that Herrick's word *youngling* is to be found in the lovely Coventry Carol. The text is that of Robert Croo, 1534: 'Lully, lulla, thou little tiny child/By by, lully lullay/O sisters too,/How we may do/For to preserve this day/This poor youngling,/For whom we do sing/By By, lully lullay.'

Dr Robert Sinclair, of Crumlin, Co. Antrim, is curious about the word *slap,* a gap in a hedge, common in north Antrim, but not in the south of that county, in Derry and Donegal, and of course in Scotland. It comes from Middle Dutch or Middle Low German *slop. Slop/slap* has been in use in Scotland for a long time. In William Dunbar's day (late 15th century) the word could mean a gap in the clouds ('The purpur hevyn our scailit in silver stoppis/Ourgilt the treis'), as well as a gap made in an opposing army: 'Stoppis their maid throu all that chewalry,/ The worthy Scottis thai wrocht so worthely.' Nowadays, the worthy Scottis and the equally worthy northern Irish have confined its use to gaps in hedges, just as Rab Burns did: 'To slink thro' slaps an' reave an' steal, At stacks o' pease,' said he in *Poor Mailie.*

Scantlin and Dick Grace

The Kilkenny man who recently wrote out for me his grandmother's recipe for a plum-based liqueur, mentioned a *scantlin* of sugar, meaning a small quantity, as the ingredient that would put a bit of life in the finished product, and, no doubt, into those venturing to have a *drigeen* (small drop) of it. An interesting word *scantlin,* and not one I've heard anywhere else in Ireland, not even in the

Norman baronies of Wexford. *Scantillon* was an earlier English form of the word and it meant a carpenter's gauge; but *scantlin*, or *scantling*, came to Kilkenny, I suspect, directly from the Old French *escantillon*, or Middle French *eschantillon*, a standard measure of weight. These words were a modification of Middle French *eschandillon*, diminutive of *escandille*, or Old Provencal *escandil*, from vulgar Latin *scandilia*, from Latin *scandere*, to climb. A long journey the word had from ancient Rome to Power's pub in Slieverue.

A recent column about the naming of certain playing cards prompts an Athlone correspondent to ask what card game the bold Colonel Grace might have been playing when he scribbled his answer to King William on the back of the six of hearts, thus giving that card the name *Dick Grace*, which is still used in parts of the midlands and the southeast. I can only hazard a guess and say that it was possibly fifteen, or one of its variants twenty five, thirty five, forty five etc. These were the most popular Irish card games at the time; some years after the Grace episode the Kerry poet Aogán Ó Rathaille referred to one of them in the line '*Ó lom an Cuireata an cluiche ar an Rí coroinneach*': 'Since the Knave has swept the game from the crowned King'—a lightly-veiled Jacobite allusion. The same reader asks the origin of the word *bridge*, as in the card game. The simple answer to that is that I don't know. But I can tell her that in the time of George III it was called *biritch*, 'apparently changed to *bridge* after the dealer's *bridging*, or passing, the declaration of trumps to his partner' (Webster). The Oxford Dictionary says that the word is probably of Levantine origin, since some form of the game appears to have been long known in the Near East. Collins hazards the guess that bridge may be connected with the Turkish *bir-üc* (an unattested phrase) meaning one-three: 'perhaps referring to the one exposed hand and the three players' hands'.

Cards

In the days not long gone when card-playing was a feature of rural life in winter evenings, people had their own special names for many of the cards. For example, the Six of Hearts was known from Westmeath down as far as south Kilkenny as *Dick Grace;* and thereby hangs a tale.

Colonel Richard Grace was Governor of Athlone for James II. The story goes that he was sent a letter by King William asking him to espouse the Orange cause in return for promises of royal favour. The letter was delivered while the Colonel was engaged in fleecing his subordinate officers at the card table, and it so enraged him that he scribbled his reply on a discard, which happened to be the Six of Hearts. What he wrote I don't know, but it must have been pretty good to place the incident so firmly in the folk memory.

The Nine of Diamonds was once widely known as *The Curse of Scotland*. Here again there is a Jacobite connection. The Dalrymples, earls of Stair, have never been popular among those who espoused the Jacobite cause. Sir John Dalrymple, who became the first earl, was one of those who offered the crown of Scotland to William and Mary at the Revolution, and as Secretary of State for Scotland, he is blamed for causing the massacre of Glencoe. He was also very influential in bringing about the Union of Scotland with England, though he didn't live to see it in place. His son, the second earl, was ambassador to France at the time of the regency of Orleans, and was a master in the arts of intrigue against the Stuarts. He was blamed more than anybody else by Bonny Prince Charlie for preserving the crown for the Hanoverian dynasty. The Dalrymples' coat of arms bore nine lozenges, or, arranged saltire-wise: the resemblance to the Nine Diamonds has given us the term, *The Curse of Scotland*.

Are you sceptical? So was I until I saw a cartoon dated 21 October 1745, which represented the Young Chevalier trying to rush a herd of cattle carrying papal curses, writs of excommunication and such like decrees across the river Tweed, with the Nine of Diamonds lying in wait on the Scottish ground before them.

Gurriers

One should always be careful when hazarding an opinion about the provenance of dialect or slang words. Even the great Partridge could at times jump to unwarranted conclusions. In this particularly dangerous area of lexicography Jack is often as good as, or better than his master; hence the fun people get out of arguing about the origin of local words. Take for example the well-known, Dublin word *gurrier*. I have heard people arguing about this word in pubs; I have heard it discussed on radio and television programmes; and many years ago the late Seamus Kelly tried to solve the problem of its provenance in 'An Irishman's Diary' in the *Irish Times*. He was convinced that the word was borrowed from their French allies by Irish soldiers in the Great War, and that *gurrier* was simply the Dublin pronunciation of *guerrier*.

Nay, nay, thrice nay!, as the late Frankie Howerd used to say. *Guerrier*, a warrior, if it ever existed in demotic French, was certainly not current in this century or in the last one. No, the answer to the problem is, I think, to be found nearer home.

In the *English Dialect Dictionary* we find the onomatopoeic *gurr* (verb), also in the form *gurrie,* to growl as a dog, to snarl, to rumble. It is also used in the compound *gurr-gurr* hence *gurrgurring* growl or a low growl or snarl; the snarl of a dog. From this word we get *gurry* (sb.), a brawl, a loud, angry, disputation, a dog-fight. The word is also found in the compound *gurry-wurry*.

The English Dialect Dictionary, it must be admitted, gives these words as Scottish English, and it does not have *gurrier*. Still, I'll chance my arm and say that the Dublin word is connected with the onomatopoeic *gurr*, and with *gurry*, and that a man who indulges in gurries, a brawler, a street-fighter is a gurrier.

In Donegal one of their words for a gurry is a *kimsil*. The word has never, as far as I know, been recorded outside that county. What, I wonder, is the provenance of *kimsil*?

The Glenswilly Decree

In Paddy Neilly's pub, at Meenbanad in the Rosses, a man told me recently about a phrase still used among the older people in that part of the world, 'to issue a Glenswilly decree'. Meenbanad is a good step from Glenswilly; evidently the phrase, like Glenswilly *poteen*, travels well. To issue this decree against somebody spelled serious trouble for him, and the origin of the phrase is interesting. Traynor, in *The English Dialect of Donegal* (1957), says that it was a warning or summons issued by the Donegal Union or Association of Poteen-makers, which was formed about 1800 to collect money due for poteen purchased. This money could not, of course, be recovered by law. The members of the Union entered houses and seized furniture, etc., in lieu of payment. Traynor says that the activities of the Union ceased about 1850 because of a tragedy.

On one of their raids the Union men seized among other items of furniture, a fine feather bed. When they arrived at the place appointed for dividing the spoils a dead child was found in the bed; the bed had evidently been hastily rolled up and carried away without being examined, and the unfortunate child was smothered on the journey. Traynor's informant in the 1950s was a schoolmaster, Mr McGeehan of Cloghan. Henry Chichester Hart (1847–1909) whose unpublished manuscripts were used by Traynor, tells us that 'laws were made independently in this county and executed rigorously amongst the people until quite recently.'

'The term, Glenswilly decree, is now used in a bullying sense, but is nearly obsolete. If a man was known to have stolen a cow or a sheep, though no one could absolutely prove it, a Glenswilly decree would soon deprive the thief of all benefit from his theft. His own cow would be flayed, or himself thrashed, or his barn fired. Not many years ago a case arose before the magistrates out of this custom. A man bought a lot of poteen and failed to pay, knowing that as it was contraband the debt was irrecoverable by law. But the man who had stilled it issued a Glenswilly decree and seized the debtor's horse by night, which he refused to give up until he was paid.'

Although the issuing of Glenswilly decrees has died out, just as killing

your own Hessian has become unfashionable in south-east Wexford, the
spoken words remain.

Kibosh

A reader from Co. Galway would like to know whether I can throw any
light on the origin of the phrase 'to put the *kibosh* on' meaning to arrange
things so that something will not occur; to put an end to something; to spoil;
to impair; to veto. The word is widely used both here in Ireland and in
America and we must note that the emphasis is placed on the second syllable
in both countries. Let's see what the experts say.

Both the *Oxford Dictionary of English Etymology* and *Webster* say that the
word's ancestry is unknown. The OED says that it is of heraldic origin, which
is no great help. In *Phrase and Word Origins*, Alfred Holt says that *kibosh* 'can
be traced to a Yiddish word formed from four consonants, representing 18
pence. When, at a small auction, an eager bidder jumped his offer to that
figure, he was said to have "put the kibosh" on his fellow bidders.'
Unfortunately Mr Holt does not tell us what the four consonants are or why
they represented 18 pence. Webster's *New World Dictionary of the American
Language* cites an unlikely Germanic possibility: why should *kiebe,* which
means 'carrion' in middle German, lead to *kibosh?* Julian Franklyn, in his
Dictionary Of Rhyming Slang, agrees with the Oxford heraldic theory,
suggesting a link with *caboshed* or *caboched.* Pádraic Column suggested that
kibosh is none other than Irish *caidhp bháis,* death cap, an execution blind-fold
in the bad old days.

The problem I have with that is that I have never read of that kind of a
caidhp bháis being used when Larry was stretched; neither can I place any
trust in the Wexford folk-etymologies that it was the '98 Yeomanry pitch-
cap, or a cloth placed on a dead person's face. Where's the evidence that
would support any of these theories?

What do I believe? At the moment I am intrigued by what an expert on
Semitic languages, my colleague Kevin Cathcart, suggested to me recently.
Kibosh, he says, may be related to the Biblical Hebrew *kabash* and the
Akkadian *kabdsu*—to tread. Note, he says, the later Hebrew usage: to press,
squeeze; to press one's face into the ground; to hide, oneself, to suppress, to
conquer. He also notes the Aramaic *kebash*: to put on the head; to close the
eyes, to set one's face against. Can this be the answer?

Americanisms

A lady from Blanchards town writes to enquire about the origin of some

American words and phrases. The first one on her list is *shenanigans*. Mary Helen Dohan, in a book called *The Making of The American Language* thinks it may be Irish in origin, and that it comes from *sionnachaim, a* word which, if it exists at all—and I doubt it—would mean 'I play the fox, I act in a cunning manner.' Dohan also suggests the 'German' *schinagle* or *schinaglen,* and the 'Spanish' *chanade,* a trick or deceit; the trouble with her German theory is that the words she mentions don't seem to exist in that language; neither can I find the 'Spanish' word in any dictionary, nor have the Hispanic scholars I've asked about the matter heard of it. Better side with Collins and say that *shenanigans* is of unknown origin.

Another word that troubles my Blanchardstown friend is *shillelagh*. It has nothing at all to do with the oak woods of Shillelagh in Co. Wicklow. The word comes from the Irish *sail éille. Sail* is a stout cudgel and *éille* is the genitive of *iall,* a thong or leash, which in the days of faction fighting was wrapped around the wrist. The formidable *sail éille* was, according to Munster songs of the 18th century, made from either blackthorn or oak.

Lastly the lady asks whether the American word *patsy,* meaning a dupe, a fall-guy, the butt of a joke, comes from Patsy, the gullible Irishman. According to some etymologists it came from the Italian *pazzo,* crazy. Others think that perhaps it was coined to describe the 16th-century Pazzi family of Florence who, silly enough to attack the Medici, was slaughtered and the corpses sent floating down the Arno. I think it unlikely that Italian Americans coined this one after a gap of five centuries. In the late 19th century *patsy* came to mean a good guy, one of the boys, and the usually reliable John Ciardi thinks that this Patsy was your decent Irishman. But soon after this, Ciardi says, Patsy became the standard Italo-American patois for the common man's name, Pasquale ('of Easter'), and it became a generic for the Italian emigrant greenhorn, a 'patsy' for the foreman who clipped his wages and added abuse for good measure. Ciardi's book is worth reading. It is called *A Browser's Dictionary,* and it was published in New York in 1980.

Early American Words

I have always had a soft spot for early American English. This is the language brought by colonists in the 17th century, and is therefore the language spoken by Shakespeare, Milton and Bunyan. This English, influenced, of course, by the arrival of fresh immigrants from Germany, Ireland and Scandinavia, and by the forced immigration of Africans through the slave trade, is the true *fons et origo* of the colourful language of the Bronx, of the streets of Philadelphia, and of the great western plains. American English shows a high degree of linguistic uniformity; the vast dialectal differences which mark the speech of Britain and Ireland are not found in the United States. This was noticed as

early as 1781 by the Scottish president of Princeton University, who wrote
that Americans 'being much more unsettled, and moving frequently from
place to place, they are not so liable to local peculiarities either in accent or
phraseology'.

Should you be interested in the fascinating history of American English I
urge you to buy *A History of the English Language*, by Albert C. Baugh and
Thomas Cable, a beautifully produced 450-page paperback from Routledge,
priced at only £12.99 sterling. The American section is just one in a scholarly
book that is a model of clarity and quite the best history of English obtainable
in one volume.

Baugh and Cable show us that American pronunciation compared with
that of London is somewhat old-fashioned. The American use of *gotten*
instead of *got* would have pleased Dr Johnson. Americans still use *mad* in the
sense *of angry*, as Shakespeare did, and as we Irish do, and their *I guess* is
certainly as old as Chaucer. Their picturesque old word *Fall* was used by
Christopher Marlowe; *Autumn* they learn from schoolbooks. They have kept
the general significance of *sick* without restricting it to nausea. So have we.
The early colonists found some words ready-made for them by the native
Americans; *wigwam, tomahawk, canoe, toboaggan, moccasin, papoose*. From their
French enemies they learned *portage, caribou, bureau* and *chowder*, from the
Germans *pretzel, noodle* and *sauerkraut*, from the Dutch *coleslaw, cookie, scow*
and *boss*. They had a gift for the imaginative phrase, and to them we owe
*to bark up the wrong tree, to face the music, fly off the handle, go on the war path,
bury the hatchet*.

The Americans have always been justly proud of their distinctive speech;
indeed Thomas Jefferson speculated that one day they would call their
language by a name other than English. Spanglish perhaps?

Ballyhoo

It is astonishing how many lexicographers trace to this beloved land of ours words
associated with outrageous, boisterous, generally uncivilised behaviour. I recently came across—in an Irish-American journal, mark you—the following
definition of the word *ballyhoo:* 'riotous uproar, Irish fashion; high-powered
vulgar publicity as practised by Irish boxing managers in former times. The word
is traceable to the County Cork village of Ballyhooly, noted for its iracible
inhabitants.' In Paul Beale's edition of Partridge's *Concise Dictionary, of Slang*,
ballyhoo is also given as an abbreviation of *ballyhooly*; the dictionary quotes the
TLS as saying in 1934 that *ballyhoo* 'is now the recognised term for eloquence
aimed at the pocket-book'. *Ballyhooly* is glossed as 'copy-writers' or politicians'
exaggeration; advanced publicity of a vulgar or misleading kind'. *Ballyhooly truth*,
we are told, is a music hall tag from circa 1880–85.

But where does the wretched word come from? Collins says that it is of uncertain origin; Oxford likewise hedges its bets; the *American World Book Dictionary* puts the blame squarely on Ballyhooly. But then comes the English lexicographer Adrian Room, in his *True Etymologies* (Routledge, 1986) to restore the good name of that blameless, peaceful place. The word is a nautical one, he thinks, and the actual derivation is *ballyhou,* a native Central American Indian name for a type of wood from which a clumsy boat was made in the great days of sail. This in turn gave way to the expression '*ballyhoo of blazes*', used contemptuously by sailors for a ship they disliked. The phrase, apparently, was still actively used in the present century. Mr Room, I hear, has holidayed in Cork. Somebody in Ballyhooly should stand him a pint, whether he's right or wrong!

My thanks to 'an old soldier, rtd.', for sending me a most interesting list of words which were for a time after the Great War common among Irish soldiers who had returned from the Indian Army. One of these is *natch,* a woman fond of dancing. *Nac* in Hindi, was a traditional dance; the word came originally from a Sanskrit word meaning dancing. My correspondent heard the word in Cobh in his youth.

Tuam Schoolboy Slang

I am grateful to the many readers who have sent me word lists for inclusion in the projected *Dictionary of Irish English*. Before you could say Tom Murphy a letter arrived from Mr Noel Donoghue of Tuam, containing a very valuable list of his town's slang words. They were published in a magazine called *The Great Tuam Annual 2*, which bears the imprint of Lions International, and sells at a deuce of lats—£2 to you. A note to the article pays tribute to the collectors, some students of St Jarlath's College, as I do now.

A penny in Tuam is a *clod-hopper,* 50 pence is a *corner;* five pounds is a *flem;* £10 is a *brick*.

Tuam has its own rhyming slang: *birdlime* is time. 'Lamp the birdlime, let's skirt' means 'look at the time, let's leave quickly'. A *bugler* is a burger; *banners* are chips (from Arran banners, I suppose); *nails* is another word for chips. Perhaps a *cackler's corie* would be more to your taste—a leg of chicken. To be *lakes* means to be insane; to *munge a budgie* means to kiss a girl. To *mug* also means to kiss. A *pineapple* is a church. A *kaedie* is a cap. To *skate* means to dance. *Skates* are shoes. A *riddle* is a toilet. A *sham* is 'a citizen of Tuam, a gentleman, an upright person'; *the ould sham* is the speaker's father; *the ould queen* is his/her mother. A *scan* is 'a person from the parish of Milltown'; not being a local, I don't know whether the word is pejorative or not; *a shaft* is 'a low type from nine miles out the road'; a *spare* is glossed as 'an unliked, ignorant person, a twillix'.

Tome is an adjective meaning 'legendary, incredible, fabulous.' A *tome feek* is an incredibly beautiful girl. *Gils* is glossed as 'a human being, the word being used solely with possessive adjective as in *my gils*=me; *your gils*=you, etc.' *Huzzes* is glossed as personal pronoun, 1st person plural—'we'. *Lettie* is a bed. To *lamp* means to look.

Perhaps I'm wrong, but the 200-word Tuam list seems to be comprised for the most part of the colourful language of youth. It is none the less valuable for that.

You Don't Say

I am Ulster; my people are an abrupt people
Who like the spiky consonants in speech.

William O'Kane of Dungannon quotes this couplet by W.R. Rodgers in his *You Don't Say,* a book modestly described by its author as 'not a dictionary as such, but an offering of a selection of dialect words as used throughout the Northern part of Ireland, together with examples of their meanings, usage and wherever possible, their derivations. Like Ben Kiely, who has written an introduction to Mr O'Kane's work, I read the book with great pleasure. This is an enchanted wood, as Kiely says, in which the imagination can run wild after dancing and fluttering words.

Where, I wonder, does the marvellous word *sprachle* come from? Mr O'Kane says that it means to flounder, to move clumsily and untidily; to clamber. 'I saw him sprachlin' through the bushes looking for his golf ball'. *Sprachled* means sprawled out. 'She was sprachled all over the sofa watching television'. *Grulch* is 'a stocky, strong fellow who is rather rough and ready in his ways, and perhaps a mite dour, but a long way this side of a *hellion*'. (A Donegal *grulch* is a very small pig, according to Traynor's lexicon.) A *hallion* is 'someone, invariably large, who is uncouth and lazy. The word is also used of anybody engaged in horseplay or rough physical behaviour'. The American *hellion* derives from *hallion*, a word common in Scotland and in the North of England in the 19th century. It then meant a tramp, a hooligan. It comes, perhaps, from the French *haillon,* a rag. Partridge has 'hallion: a shrew'.

What, think you, is a *cuckoo's lachtar*? To the Tyrone man it means an only child. *Lachtar* is the Irish for a clutch of eggs.

Reputable scholars have estimated that a glossary of 2,000 words would be required to enable a modern literate Englishman to read Shakespeare, but that 200 words or less would be all that a North of Ireland person would need. Mr O'Kane's book contains many forgotten Tudor words. *Colly* is a small soot particle in coal dust. In Shakespeare's time *to colly* meant to blacken. We find 'brief as the lightning in the collied night' in *A Midsummer Night's Dream*.

You Don't Say (161 pp.) was published by the Irish World in Dungannon in 1991 at £5.95. As far as I know it is out of print. I hope that Mr O'Kane will soon give us a second—and perhaps enlarged—edition of his splendid book.

Chimneys

A very interesting letter has arrived from a townland at the foot of Mount Leinster, on the Carlow side. The reader asks whether two local variants of the word 'chimney' are to be found elsewhere in the country—*chimbley* and *chimlay*. Well, I've heard *chimbley* in many's the place, and *chimlay* from itinerants, natives of, or *agree to,* as they say in Kilmore Quay, Counties Wicklow and Wexford. The English Dialect Dictionary gives variants from England, Scotland and Wales: *chembly, chimberley, chimbley, chimdy, chimla, chimler* (England); *chimblay, chimbla, chumbla* (Wales); *chimbla, chimley, chambley* (Scotland). We in Ireland may have as many variants. I'd like to know what they are, and where they are found.

The word 'chimney' has a long and interesting history, and fascinating associations. It derives from Greek *kaminos,* fireplace, oven, furnace. The Latin was *caminus,* which gave Late Latin *caminata,* which in turn gave Old French *cheminée,* which begot the Irish *simné,* the English *chimney,* and its various dialect forms. Chimneys as we know them were a late medieval development and they were blamed for many disastrous fires. This led to the imposition of curfews (Old French *cuevrefeu,*—'cover the fire').

The Romans called the fireplace *focus,* a hearth or brazier under a hole in the roof. The English focus, the point at which sight lines meet, follows, because the Roman's focus was the place where people were drawn to warm themselves.

The Romans had another interesting word, *fornix,* a vault, from which 19th century biologists derived *fornicate,* to be arched or hoodlike in form. But as to the old Roman vaults, in them the working girls laid down their mattresses and fornicated like the divil's father. They were of course, denounced loudly by the early Christians for what they got up to: thus was the sin named after the occasion of sin.

Bailey's Dictionary

One of the most amusing dictionaries ever written in English was the very first one to consider the origins of words, Nathaniel Bailey's *An Universal Etymological Dictionary,* published in 1721. I was allowed look at it when I was a student in Trinity in Old God's Time. All I remember about it is that Mr Bailey was hilariously inventive, but alas, the notes I took at the time I have since lost. It is a notable work, the first to stress the importance of the provenance of words, and its readability brought it to bestseller status. Dr Johnson seems to have taken Bailey at face value. He drew a lot of water from Bailey's well when compiling his own famous Dictionary. Johnson (his doctorate came from TCD) needed no lessons in inventiveness when it came to etymology: he derived *helter-skelter* from the Old English for 'the darkness of hell, hell being a place of confusion'. He was not very amused when a young Irish wag informed him that he had got it wrong, and that the compound came from the Latin *hilariter celeriter;* cheerfully swiftly. It didn't, of course; it is an echoic reduplication, like hurry-scurry.

What about *namby-pamby?* Johnson hasn't got it, although it was current in his time. There seems to be unanimity among scholars as to its provence. It came into being through the process of rhyming reduplication from the petname Nam, short for Ambrose, the Ambrose in question, Ambrose Phillips, (died 1749) being a poet of no great merit who wrote, well, namby-pamby pastoral verse in imitation of Virgil. He was convinced that his immorality as a pastoral poet was secure, and that he would be remembered. He was right, in a way, the poor man.

Jackson

Our most eminent lexicographer, Professor Tomás de Bhaldraithe, has, I see, persuaded Collins's *English Dictionary,* to which he is special consultant editor on matters pertaining to Irish English, to include words of Irish provenance in their original garb. *Poitín* is there, as well as *poteen, báinín* as well as *bawneen; crios* he has sensibly left alone as nobody has yet mutilated the word by providing it with an anglicised spelling. *Jackeen* has now been promoted from dialect to standard English; the Collins definition is: 'a slick, self-assertive, lower-class Dubliner'.

The application of the term 'jackeen' was not confined to native Dubliners in pre-Famine times, however. Mr and Mrs Samuel Carter Hall described the jackeen as he was in the early 1840s in their *Ireland, Its Scenery And Character.* He belonged to the lowest rank of society.

The prejudice in favour of 'birth', the Halls tell us, then pervaded all ranks, 'and the numbers of idlers in the busy world is fearfully large; from the "walking gentleman" of the upper ranks, to the "half-sir" of the middle, and the "Jackeen" of the class a little above the lower; the "walking gentleman" being always elegantly attired, and of course always unemployed, with ample leisure for the studies which originate depravity; the "half-sir" being, generally a younger brother, with little or no income of his own, and so educated as to be deprived, utterly, of the energy and self-dependence which create usefulness; the "Masther Tom" who broke the dogs, shot the crows, first backed the vicious horse, and, followed by a half-pointer, half-lurcher; poached secretly upon his elder brother's land, but more openly upon the land of his neighbours; the "Jackeen" being a production found everywhere, but most abundantly in large towns.

'Happily, however, the class is not upon the increase. The "Jackeen" might have been seen—regularly a few years ago, and now occasionally—at early morning lounging against the Trinity College rails, with the half-in-toxicated, half-insolent air that betokens a night passed in debauch; his stockings, that had once been white, failing from under the drab-green, ill-fitting trousers over the shoes; his coat usually of green; his waistcoat of some worn and faded finery; and the segment of collar that peeped over the stock, fashionable in cut, but not in quality, was crushed and degraded from its original property; his hat, always a little on one side, had a knowing "bend" over the right eye; one of his arms was passed, with that peculiar affectation of carelessness which evinces care, through the rails, and brought round, so as to enable the hand to shift the coarse and bad cigar that rested on his lip—there was a torn glove upon the other; and his dull bloodshot eyes winked impudently upon every girl that passed'.

Mockt

The lifeboatman to whom I was talking in the public house in Kilmore Quay turned away to say good night to a friend, sweeping a pint and a half-one from the table behind us with his coat-tail. His apology to the young couple whose drink he had spilled ended with the excuse that all day there had been a *mockt* on him.

Ó Dónaill's Irish-English dictionary has the word *macht,* a transitive verb, meaning kill, slaughter, in literary usage. The Royal Irish Academy's *Diction-ary of the Irish Language,* based mainly on Old and Middle Irish material, gives *macht* as a noun, possibly meaning destruction, and probably an abstraction from *machtaid* a loanword from the Latin *mactare,* to slay, smite, afflict, punish. Here I suppose, was the origin of the Kilmore man's affliction, hoodoo or jinx.

But what, I wonder, is the origin of the predominantly Australian slang expressions, to put the mock, or mocker, or mockers on somebody or something, meaning to put a jinx on them? Every authority on Australian slang I've consulted say that the words *mock, mocker* and *mockers* are of Hebrew origin. (*Makkah* means plague; plural *makkot.* The words come from a root word meaning to strike.) One scholar, Beale, quotes a private source as identifying the words as market traders' argot which might, he thinks, possibly indicate continuity from 19th-century London Jewish traders.

I wonder. Jewish traders in 19th-century London spoke Yiddish, not

Hebrew, and a colleague of mine who searched Yiddish dictionaries for me found no word that resembles the Australian slang words.

So. I'm left wondering whether the Australian words are really the legacy of Jewish people, or an Irish cultural export, deriving from the Anglo Irish *mockt,* itself a child of the Irish *macht.* I reserve judgement. If only we could ask the opinion of those who left these shores somewhat reluctantly in the early years of the last century! What an informant on language the balladeer who left with the following witty lines on his lips would have been.

> And is it not uncommon fly
> Of them that rules the nation
> To make us end with Botany
> Our public education?

Political Correctness or Plain Lunacy

I have just read *The Official Politically Correct Dictionary and Handbook* by Henry Beard and Christopher Cerf (Grafton, 176 pp. £5 stg) and great gas it is. Dear me, to think that people were once pronounced dead, not 'terminally inconvenienced', or 'metabolically different' as suggested by the University of California at Berkeley? Once upon a time people grew old, and not 'experientially enhanced'; they got drunk and not chemically inconvenienced'. They used such demeaning words as 'disease' instead of the sensitive word 'condition'.

Would you believe that some old academic fogies have objected to the proposal that the Four Horsemen of the Apocalypse should be renamed Nutritional Deprivation, State of Belligerency, Widespread Transmittable Condition and Terminal Inconvenience? Would you believe that some people still favour that nasty word, murder, instead of the term designated for use in US State department reports by Assistant Secretary of State Elliot Abrams back in 1984 in relation to friendly governments like Chile and El Salvador—'arbitrary deprivation of life'; and that insensitive phrases such as 'airplane crash' are still commonly used instead of that favoured by the US National Safety Transportation Board, 'controlled flight into terrain.'

I hope that you don't correct your child, as some parents do, when he tells you that 2+2=5; the child is not wrong, merely 'differently logical'.

Are you still, by any chance, using woman instead of 'wofem', the substitute proposed by the redoubtable Bina Goldfield, author of *The Efemcipated English Handbook*? This wofem has also given us the following beauties: abdofem, afemdfemt, comfemcefemt, femagefemt. 'I decline to ovarify,' the wofem declared, on the basis of my Fifth Afemdfemt rights.' You think experientially enhanced Bina is emotionally different? Well then, try 'womyn', recommended by *Random House Webster's College Dictionary* both as an alternate spelling of 'women', and as a singular. You might also try 'wimmin', 'wimyn', (sing.) 'womban', 'womon' (pl.).

This dictionary is a well-researched and highly entertaining account of current (mainly American) attempts on the life of the English language. A great buy, if you can womage the fiver.

Postures

'The Grecian bend', a posture for which the girleen in the song 'The Garden Where the Praties Grow' showed such laudable disdain, is troubling a reader from rural Co. Kildare. 'What exactly is this Grecian bend?' she asks, adding that having had to listen to her husband's celebrated imitation of the late Count McCormack's rendering of the song every Saturday night for the past 30 years, she has begun to wonder if the affliction was induced by drink.

Partridge, in the *Macmillan Dictionary of Historical Slang*, is the only scholar I can find who has something to say about this phrase. It was, he says, a stoop affected in walking by many women 1869–90. He says the *Daily Telegraph* used the phrase in the 1860s, and that it was anticipated by the *The Etonian* as early as 1821. That journal used it of a scholarly stoop, however. By 1874 *Grecian bend* had become milliners' slang for an exaggerated bustle (dress improver).

The 19th century seems to have been a great time for all sorts of affected walking habits. Apart from the *Grecian bend* there was the *Alexandra Limp*— nothing to do with the Dublin school of great fame, but a walk affected by society ladies, circa 1865–80, as a compliment to the Princess of Wales. London and Dublin ladies who belonged to a society unknown to Her Royal Highness often had recourse to the *Tout's Twist*. *Tout* was a word in cant use as far back as the 16th century. It meant the buttocks.

The men had their own style while the ladies were limping, stooping and twisting their touts. The fashionable young man's gait of the mid-century, first seen in London and immediately copied, of course, in Dublin, was the *Roman Fall,* an extraordinary posture in walking, in which the head was thrown well forward while the small of the back was pulled well in. This was affected by the young gent on his best behaviour, anxious to impress the limpers and stoopers, not the tout twisters. When the older swingers wanted to impress the more, shall we say spirited young females, they frequently adopted the *Roo Roll*, considered to be a sexy, indeed lascivious saunter, in which the head was kept well back, and the pelvis thrust out while the hips were rolled. *Roo* was mid-19th slang for a rake (Fr. *roué*). Go on, have fun! But mind the old back.

Culinary Words

A lady from Seattle who has settled down in Donegal wants to know the origin of some of our culinary words. The first is *spud*.

Back in the 15th century a *spudde* was a short knife *or* dagger with a fairly wide blade. There seems to be no mention of the thing in the literature of the 16th century, but we find it in the 17th: 'a spade-like instrument for weeding and digging'. In the 19th century it was applied to the crop it was formerly used to harvest.

Next is *colcannon*. The word is an interesting mixture, as is the dish. The first bit, *col,* is from Irish *cál,* kale or cabbage, but we borrowed the word from the Old Norse *kál.* Piers the Plowman ate *cawel* or *caul,* the Welsh ate *cawl,* Rembrandt ate *kool,* while his German friends ate *kohl,* earlier *cholo,* or *kol.* All these words have their roots in the Latin *caulis,* later *caulus,* stem, stalk, cabbage. The *cannon* part of the word is Irish *ceanann,* white-tipped, speckled with white, a reference, needless to say, to the potatoes in the dish.

My correspondent asks me whether *sowans* are still eaten in Ireland. I doubt it. Paddy the Cope mentioned that the dish was popular among the Donegal labourers in the bad old days. Sowans are the inner husks of oats, winnowed and threshed, which were fermented in salted water, then drained, and the mess boiled up as a porridge. This was a popular dish around the feast of *Samhain,* the great pagan feast that was superseded by All Souls; the dish takes its name from the feast.

Brotchan Foltchep is how my correspondent refers to her final dish. This should be written *brachán foltchíbe,* a delicious northern oatmeal and leek soup, just the thing for hungry kids now that winter is icumen in. *Brachán* is oatmeal porridge, *foltchíb* is leek. Here's the recipe, courtesy of the late Theodora Fitzgibbon, who got it near Churchill, Co. Donegal, my correspondent tells me. 'Cut six large leeks into chunks an inch long. Heat 4 cups of milk with a heaped tablespoon of butter, and when boiled add 2 tablespoons of oatmeal. Let it boil, add the chopped leeks and season with salt and pepper. Simmer for 45 minutes. Add a tablespoon of chopped parsley and boil again for a few minutes. Enjoy.'

Borrowings

It is strange, isn't it, how words change meaning as they move from one language to another. The Latin *bestia,* beast, gave Italian *biscia,* but that word means a snake; it gave English *bitch,* French *bische,* but that means a female deer; and it gave Portuguese *bicho,* which means an insect. It is equally strange how borrowed phrases survive in the new language and go out of fashion in the old: the French no longer use *nom de plume, double entendre, panache, bon viveur* or *legerdemain,* and I don't think I've ever seen R.S.V.P. on a French invitation card: always *prière de répondre.*

It is strange, too, how modern European languages tend to do the oddest things with English participles, so that you won't find many French people running or jogging; they prefer to go *footing.* Neither is sunbathing very popular, it seems: *le bronzing* is, however. A friend of mine was a little confused recently when he was advised by a Parisian lady to be sure to wear *un smoking;* she meant a dinner jacket. In Italy, I'm told, cosmetic surgeons have begun to refer to their craft as *il lifting.* Swedish, too, has come under the English influence and Professor Magnus Ljung of Stockholm wrote recently that more than half of all Swedes now make plurals by adding *-s,* after the English model, rather than by adding *-ar,* or *-er,* in the usual Swedish way.

I mentioned recently that the French have, since 1911, been taking action against the encroachment of foreign words; I was amused to find—thanks to a cutting sent to me by a London reader—that the *Daily Mail,* in 1945, was advocating that the British press refuse to print American words 'that are positively incomprehensible to the average English person.' These included *commuter, rare,* as applied to undercooked meat; *seafood;* dumb, meaning stupid; *mean* in the sense of nasty; *intern; dirt road;* and, horror of horrors, *livingroom!*

In 1986 *The Economist* amused itself by conducting a survey to find out which English words have become truly international, comprehensible to people all over the world. The list they published was remarkably short: *airport, passport, hotel, telephone, bar, soda, cigarette, sport, golf, tennis, stop, OK, weekend, jeans, know-how, sex-appeal, no problem.* They concluded: 'The presence of so many words to do with travel, consumables and sport attests to the real source of these exports—America.'

Shakespeare and the Computer

In recent years computers have been put to good use by scholars who fed them not alone the complete Works of Shakespeare but the complete works of every author who wrote in English before and during the lifetime of the man from Stratford. From this operation it was found that Shakespeare had a vocabulary of 17,677 words, at least 10% of which had never been seen in print before, and some scholars have concluded that he had coined the entire 10%. Perhaps they are right in this, but I think it likely that some of these may have been dialect words peculiar to Shakespeare's own district, and probably unknown outside it; indeed the Danish scholar, Jespersen, had concluded in pre-computer days (*Growth and Structure of the English Language,*

Oxford 1905) that between 200 and 300 words in the earlier plays which Shakespeare never repeated were provincialisms that came into the language independently later, among them *cranny, beautified, homicide, aggravate, forefathers*.

Be that as it may, what a treasury of new words the poet has bequeathed us. Bryson and Morrow in their excellent study, *Mother Tongue* (New York 1990) include *critical, leapfrog, monumental, barefaced, castigate, majestic, obscene, frugal, radiance, dwindle, countless, submerged, excellent, fretful, gust, hurry, hint, lonely, summit, pedant, gloom, snow-white, fragrant, brittle*.

And what a phrasemaker he was! The computer people back up the American scholars in confirming that he was solely responsible for *in my mind's eye; one fell swoop; more in sorrow than in anger; to be in a pickle; bag and baggage; vanish into thin air; budge an inch; play fast and loose; go down the primrose path; remembrance of things past; the sound and the fury; cold comfort; salad days; to beggar all description; flesh and blood; foul play; tower of strength* etc. etc.

By means of the computer it has also been confirmed that Ben Jonson was the writer who first used *defunct, damp, clumsy* and *strenuous;* that Sir Thomas More gave the world *absurdity, acceptance, exact, explain, and exaggerate;* that Sir Thomas Elyot, the classicist, coined *exhaust, animate* and *modesty,* and that Newton coined *centrifugal* and *centripetal;* that Coleridge was responsible for *intensify,* Jeremy Bentham for *international,* and Carlyle for *decadent* and *environment*. Among the coinages that did not survive were Shakespeare's *barky, vastidity* and *tortive;* Ben Jonson's *ventositous* and *obstupefact,* Milton's *inquisiturient* and Dickens's *vocular*. The fun, the computer boys tell me, is only beginning.

Brass Monkeys

A reply to a letter from somebody who lives in lovely Ringabella, Co. Cork, calls for a certain amount of delicacy; the query, you see, is about the origin of a well known phrase connected with the effects of hyperborean weather on a brass monkey.

Because of a lack of printed evidence, the safest thing to say about this expression is that it is of uncertain age and origin. Some respected naval historians have said that there is merit in the suggestion that it dates from the 17th century, when cannon balls were stacked on metal trays called *monkeys*. These were usually made of iron, but on some ships brass monkeys were used. They contained shallow, saucer-shaped receptacles and these kept each cannon ball from sliding about. In fair weather a pyramid could be made, building on this secure foundation. But trouble arose in extremely cold weather, when a different coefficient of expansion led to the brass monkeys contracting quicker than the iron, causing the collapse of the pyramid. As the old story tellers used to say, *má tá bréag ann bíodh—ní mise a chum ná a cheap é,* if there's a lie in it, so be it; I wasn't the one who made it up!

My friend, Wexford author Richard Roche, writes to ask whether the common malediction *bad cess to you* is Irish in origin. It is indeed. *Collins* dates the curse from the 19th century, when *cess* had become a slang word for luck, and was used by such notables as Miss Edgeworth, Griffin, Carleton, and Mrs Anna Maria Hall who knew Mr Roche's country so well; but its origin lay in the 16th century, when *cess* meant the obligation to provide the soldiers and household of the lord deputy with supplies at fixed prices. In 17th- and 18th-century Ireland the word was used to denote any military exaction.

The origin of the word *bankrupt* puzzles Mrs Henderson from Coleraine. Her dictionary tells her that it comes from the Italian *banca rotta.* What, she wants to know, has a broken bench to do with being bankrupt? Well, in the middle ages, banking was conducted in the market place, al fresco. When a banker became insolvent his bench was broken up. Simple as that. Isn't it strange, by the way, how the term *al fresco* has lost its original meaning in demotic Italian? The Italians still use it, but nowadays to them it signifies not being outside, but in jail!

A Bee in His Bonnet

Mrs J. Bryson who lives in Belfast, wants to know the origin of the phrase 'He has a bee in his bonnet'. Partridge, incredibly, says that the phrase was obsolete by 1900, and he has little else to add, except to say that it was in vogue in the 17th. century. John Heywood, in his compilation of English proverbs, printed in 1546, has 'bees in the head'. There was an old belief that anxiety and restlessness could be caused by insects—earwigs, for instance—boring through the ear into the brain; perhaps the bee was also blamed. I don't know who first put the bee in the *bonnet,* but the idiom was known to Robert Herrick, to judge from his *Mad Maud's Song,* published in 1648:

Ah! woe is me, woe, woe is me.
Alack and well-a-day!
For pity, sir, find out that bee
Which bore my love away!
I'll seek him in your bonnet brave,
I'll seek him in your eyes.

As we are on the subject of idiom, another Belfast reader, Mr George Reid, wants to know the origin of the phrase 'dog tired'. He wonders whether it has anything to do with 'the exhaustion of hard-driven huskies in the far north'. I don't think so. *Dog* was not an unusual prefix in

Elizabethan times, used as an emphatic substitute for 'very'. Offhand I can think of only two other examples: Shakespeare's *dog cheap* in Henry IV, Part One; and Thomas Kydd's *dog rough,* in *The Spanish Tragedy*—an expression still in common use. The word is of Norse origin (cf. Swedish *dag,* very).

A card from Aherlow, Co. Tipperary, asks for information about the uncommon word *leaing-gó-lí* or *lang-go-lee,* a word used in both the Irish and English of Muskerry, in West Cork. My correspondent has it from a line in a spoof hunting song: 'bhí Róidí Arthur is a leaing-gó-lí ann'. It is an imitative formation and it means (a) a weaver, that is a horse who continually sways from side to side while standing in his stable, considered a serious fault; (b) a horse whose lazy gait while walking is that of a weaver, as much a side-to-side motion as a forward one; (c) *membrum virile pendens.* The word is probably related to the Irish *longar,* noun, a swaying, rocking motion, itself, I'd say, related to English *languor,* Old French *langour,* from Latin *languor.*

Earwigs and Other Creatures

A reference to that obnoxious creature, the earwig, in a recent column led to a letter from Cavan and another from Tyrone. My Cavan reader tells me that the insect is known as *buggadawheetyeen* in his place; while my Strabane friend knows it as *tethery erse.* Estyn Evans called the *earwig* 'the lexicographer's darlinng , and no wonder. In the province of Ulster alone 83 words for the creature have been recorded, and here are some of them: *Eariwig; dheel* (Irish *daol*); *deelawg; doolog; coolygoleen* (Irish *cuileog an lin-flax fly*); *gollagoleen, gullygleen; gullioneel; gall; gellock; geelick; geelogue, geelybug, gallan-picker, gullacher; horny gollach; forkie-tail; clipshear; hedge clock; clothes creeper; jet; sissywig; scodgible.* I am indebted to the late Dr John Braidwood of Queen's University for these, published in *The Ulster Dialect Lexicon,* in 1975. *Daol* is particularly interesting. In dialects insect names, like bird and plant names, tend to be applied to different species, and *daol* is normally applied to the *devil's coach* (staphylinus olens). Braidwood gave us a bit of Cavan folklore concerning this ugly insect, not only because folklore relieves the drudgery of lexicography, but because it was his belief that dialect should be studied in the full context of folklife.

When Our Lord was being pursued by His enemies He passed one day through a field where some men were sowing corn. Next day the corn was ripe, and the reapers were asked by Our Lord's pursuers if He had passed their way. They replied that He had passed when they were sowing the corn. The *daol,* it is said then pointed with his tail in the direction in which He went. The story may condone an Irish rhymester's cruelty who declared, 'Is fearr daol a loscadh ná Aoine ag troscadh'—it is better to burn a daol than to fast on a Friday.

Braidwood also mentioned some taboo terms. To the fishing folk of Kilkeel, Co. Down, *freety* (superstitious) like all fishing communities, the following words are taboo: *nun, priest, pig, bacon, ham, hare, rat* and *salmon.* Disaster could be averted by saying *cold iron* or *heavy metal.* The salmon was referred to as *the cold iron man.* These taboos were, of course, connected with non-linguistic *freets* like the efficacy of iron; turning back if a rat or a red-haired woman crossed your path; lashing two boats together to avoid being third out of a harbour; inviting a storm by whistling on board ship.

Tell It to the Marines

A Dublin lady who is married to an ex-US Marine writes to ask me to settle an argument about the provenance of the phrase, *Tell that to the marines.* The lady thinks the phrase originated in America; her husband thinks it is English in origin, and in this he is correct. Partridge traces it back to 1806 to a book called *The Post Captain.* He also quotes Byron: 'That will do for the marines but the sailors won't believe it.' I mentioned the problem to an old salt at the recent launching of the new lifeboat in Kilmore Quay, and he kindly lent me *Salty Dog Talk,* a little book on the nautical origin of everyday expressions by two naval historians, Bill Beavis and Richard McCloskey (Adlard Coles Nautical, London). They tell us that Samuel Pepys, the diarist and Secretary to the Royal Navy, was scoffed at by courtiers when he told Charles II about flying fish seen by his friend, the captain of HMS *Defyance.* One of those present, however, Sir William Killigrew, insisted that flying fish did exist; he had seen them himself. The king then remarked: 'From the nature of their calling no class of our subjects can have so wide a knowledge of the seas and lands as the Officers and Men of our Loyal Maritime Regiment. Henceforth ere we cast doubts upon a tale that lacks likelihood, we will first tell it to the marines!'

It is obvious that Jack Tar turned the phrase subsequently; since then it has become the classic statement of disbelief.

My Country, Right or Wrong

A reader from Cork wants to know the origin of the phrase 'My country, right or wrong'. This gung-ho phrase was first uttered by the American naval hero Stephen Decatur in 1816. Decatur's Toast, as it is known in Annapolis and Westpoint circles, prompted Chesterton to write in *The Defendant* (1901): ' "My country right or wrong" is a thing that no patriot would think of saying, except in a desperate case. It is like saying 'My mother, drunk or sober".'

My friend David Hammond from Belfast won't be too pleased with my tardiness in answering his query regarding the origin of the phrase 'to send someone to Coventry', meaning to refuse to speak to a person. There are almost as many theories about this one as there are dictionaries of phrases; but I would discount the lot in favour of the origin suggested in Nigel Ree's engaging—and scholarly—*Dictionary of Phrase and Allusion* (Bloomsbury, 1992). Rees claims that the phrase may have originated in the England of the Civil War. When captured Royalists were sent to Coventry, a strongly Roundhead town, they were bound to have suffered serious discrimination. This would appear to be supported by a passage in Clarendon's *History of the Rebellion* (1702–4): 'Birmingham, a town so wicked that it had risen upon small parties of the King's men, and killed or taken them prisoners and sent them to Coventry.'

Finally, a query from Killester about the word *scumber*, 'a real Dublin working-class word'. The late Beatrice Behan gave me the word a couple of years ago. Brendan, she told me, used it as both a verb and a noun. I noted from her: 'to scumber: to make an absolute mess of the job; scumber, noun, a thoroughly messed-up job'. The English Dialect Dictionary gives: 'scumber, verb, Cornwall, of a bird, to discharge excrement'. Massinger uses the word in *The Picture*. 'When the hounds are led out to scumber'. The origin of this good word is Old French, *escombrer,* to clean out. Dermot Morgan used a cognate word, scumbling, in a radio interview with Gay Byrne last year. Scumbling, he said, means making a mess of a painting job, if my memory serves me correctly. How good it is that these words of Norman origin survive in the speech of working-class Dubliners.

Love and Deuce, Hijack

What the old-ballad maker called *creasa an tsamhraidh,* or the sparks of Summer, prompted a reader in Manorhamilton, Co. Leitrim, to write seeking information about the history of a few sporting terms. These are connected with tennis—*love* and *deuce.* A popular folk etymology asserts that *love* in tennis comes from the French *l'oeuf,* the egg. It doesn't I'm afraid. In tennis scores the French say, and have always said *zero* for nothing; and French slang has never used egg for *zero.* Neither does it come from the 'O' symbol once used in sentimental letter-writing; the 'O' represented a hug, while 'X' represented a kiss. It comes from 'love' as it was used in the expression 'play for love', that is play for nothing, or, without stakes. Bear in mind the phrase 'labour of love' which is work done for nothing.

As for deuce, which means that the score is forty all, this does come from the Old French *deux,* Modern French *deux,* because to win the game a player must score two successive points.

Jane O'Regan from Cork wants to know what the origin of the word *hijack* is. She finds it amusing that all the major dictionaries hide behind the old reliable 'origin unknown', while being quite certain about its date, the 20th century. The Oxford Supplement dates the word from the Prohibition Era in America, ignoring Partridge, who cites it in his *Dictionary of the Underworld;* it was, he proves, in American hobo use in 1914, with the sense 'to rob men at night while they are asleep'. But as to the word's origin, not a clue do the lexicographers give. It took an amateur, the American broadcaster, John Ciardi, to find the answer. Knowing that the word was used widely in the days when speedboats carrying illegal liquor were robbed in American waters, he asked about words the Chinese, who were good at this sort of thing, might have in their vocabulary. David Ray, a Chinese expert, pointed out to him that *hoi* means ocean and that *ts'ák* means pirate. And as a further confirmation Professor Ray cited the Sino-Japanese sea term *kaizoku* or *haizoku,* pirate, which is rendered by the same characters as *hoi ts'ák.* OED, Collins, et alia, please copy.

Slang

'Slang', wrote Carl Sandburg 'is a language that takes off its coat, spits on its hands and gets to work.' An earlier American, Walt Whitman, was even more enthusiastic: 'Slang is the wholesome fermentation or eructation of those processes eternally active in language, by which the froth and specks are thrown up, mostly to pass away, though occasionally to settle and permanently crystallize'.

I would urge the person who wrote to me from the United States embassy requesting information about Afro-American slang to have a look at a journal called *American Speech,* published by the University of Alabama Press since 1925. I can also recommend *The Dictionary of Contemporary Slang* (1992), compiled by Jonathon Green (Pan Books). This book, though of English provenance, contains many examples of brand-new words coined by black Americans, most of them witty and pungent, and deserving of the immortality they shall be denied, given the ephemeral nature of slang.

Mr Green has added no fewer than a thousand new words to his 1984 edition. I have no fault at all to find with his extraordinary one-man-show except that I wish he had given us more etymological information. His book deals, in the main, with current slang, but the fact that he uses such sources as J.C. Hotten's 1859 *Dictionary of Modern Slang, Cant and Vulgar Words* goes to show that some slang words do survive to become 'respectable' parts of the lexicon. His voluminous vocabulary of the very newest *sub rosa* words and phrases is important. What, for example, would it mean to you if you were asked were you one of Dorothy's friends?

A Waterford woman who wishes to remain anonymous wants to know the origin of the word *scran* as used in the local malediction *bad scran* to you! That particular curse was common up the river in my part of Wexford in my youth, and as far as I know is still in wide use in south-east Leinster, if not in other parts of Ireland. *Scran, a* very old dialect word, means poor quality food, and together with *scrannel* (*el* being a diminutive) *scranny* and *scrawny* derives from the language of the boys who built Reginald's Tower. There is a Norwegian dialect word *skran,* meaning thin, dry. I am glad to know that the Viking influence survives in Ballybricken.

Punnin, Hessians and Naked Truth

Mr John Dowling, who lives somewhere in deepest Waterford, writes to inquire whether I have heard of the word *punnin*—not punning, meaning a play on words, but a noun meaning 'a comely, cuddly, graceful, shapely young woman', according to my correspondent. I have heard the word, Mr Dowling, and in your own county, but I am delighted to be reminded of it, because I had forgotten it.

My correspondent recently heard the word in a tavern near Cappoquin, in an encomium delivered by an ageing, tired and emotional member of the agricultural community on seeing the late Marilyn Monroe adorning the television screen in the corner of the bar.

Punnin, as my correspondent spells it, is the Irish word *punann,* a sheaf. I am not sure whether Miss Monroe would have regarded being compared to a sheaf of wheat or barley or oats as a compliment; but if you consider the matter, there is that lovely golden head, the perfect symmetrical body, the slim waist. Yes, *punnin* has to be *punann* in thin disguise. *Punann,* as Mr Niall Tóibín once remarked to me, is the lowest form of wheat!

From Miss June Murphy from Raheny comes a query about the origin of a catchphrase she heard in the South of my own county, Wexford. The phrase is 'Kill your own Hessian', and it is employed to make it quite clear that one does not want one's thunder stolen. The origin of the sanguineous phrase can be found in more than one memoir written after the 1798 rebellion; and several correspondents refer to it in the manuscripts of the Department of Irish Folklore in UCD.

One account says: 'The Hessians were notoriously bloodthirsty. It happened that after one engagement a young officer found himself detached from his troops, not far from Foulks' Mills. He drew rein at a cottage door to inquire how he could safely get to Wexford, and he was invited in by a young woman, who bade him sit down and have a refreshing drink of buttermilk.

'Along with the buttermilk she produced a pistol. She was interrupted in

her design by a pikeman who had seen the cavalry horse outside. To his offer
to do the bloody business for her, she dismissed him saying: "Be off with
you! Go kill your own Hessian." The phrase "kill your own Hessian" is
commonly used still.'

From a reader in Drumbracken, Co. Monaghan, comes a query as to the
origin of the phrases 'an fhírinne lom' and its English counterpart, 'the naked
truth'. Well, the dictionaries of phrases I have looked at suggest that these
derive ultimately from an old fable. Falsehood and Truth went for a swim,
and Falsehood stole Truth's clothes from the river-bank. Truth, that decent
man, would not wear Falsehood's clothes, and walked home in his pelt. I
would suggest, however, that the phrases may be traced to Horace's
marvellous encomium on Quintilius Varus, who died in 24 BC (*Odes*, book
one, poem 24). The dead Roman is referred to, among other things, as *nuda
veritas*. Take your pick, Mr Fitzsimons.

A lady from Sutton wrote to tell me that in her youth she often heard
young fellows referring to the women who stood apart from the men in a
dance hall as the *bevy*. She would like to know where the word came from,
and wonders whether it was a term of disparagement.

This collective noun was applied to women as far back as the 15th century,
and in the 16th Spenser referred to 'this bevie of ladies bright' in *The
Shephearde's Calendar*. *Bevy* today can mean a flock of quail or a herd of
roebuck, but what did it mean in Spenser's time? In that same 16th century
Thomas Nashe informed us that 'The terme is taken of larkes'. A beautiful,
complimentary term, if ever I heard one, and I'm glad it has survived in north
Dublin.

Me Oul Segosha

I am grateful to Mr Paddy Weston of Lusk, Co Dublin, for a valuable list of
North Dublin words, compiled by a friend of his, Paddy O'Neill, a
schoolmaster who died some twenty years ago. North Dublin, as the world
knows, is a special place on the map of Irish linguistics; an ancient dialect of
English survived there until the early 18th century—a dialect very like that
which survived in the baronies of Forth and Bargy until the beginning of the
19th.

Among Mr O'Neill's words is *sagosha*. In North Dublin the word was
formerly applied to children only, and this fact makes the schoolmaster's gloss
on it all the more interesting. It is tempting to speculate, as Mr O'Neill did,
that here we have another word adapted from a French phrase, in this instance
one heard by soldiers during the Great War, perhaps *mon cher gosse*—my dear
child.

Some of the adaptations made from the French during that terrible war are very interesting. And in case you consider the Lusk schoolmaster's gloss far-fetched, consider the phrase a colleague of mine frequently heard in his youth in Wales. If, for instance, somebody spilled tea on his neighbour's fine linen tablecloth, she would say *'saint fairy Anne'*—meaning, it doesn't matter. She didn't speak French; had she done so she would have said *cela ne fait rien*.

I am not so sure about Mr O'Neill's gloss on *sagosha*. There is another theory, advanced, I'm told, by Hugh Leondard in a newspaper article some years ago: could it have come from the Irish *seo dhuitse,* which means 'here— for you'? How could it, you might well ask, and where's the connection? Consider this, The first Monday in the New Year was called both *Handsel Monday* and *Suggit Monday* in the Liberties of Dublin and in other parts of Leinster in days gone by. (Irish was spoken in parts of the Liberties until the 1830s.) On that day children called on their neighbours and on the shops their mothers dealt in demanding their *suggit;* a word derived from the Irish *seo dhuit,* the phrase that accompanied the gift. I accept that it is entirely possible that English speakers could have adapted the phrase; and note that the Lusk schoolmaster told us that *segosha* was a word used only when speaking to children in the rare oul times.

Some Phrases and a Shambles

'He'd steal the coppers off the eyes of the dead' runs a phrase I overheard recently in Wicklow. I had long thought that the custom of placing pennies on a dead person's eyes was an Irish one, but I recently read a poem by Karl Shapiro prophesying the death of Franklin D. Roosevelt which has the couplet: 'With coins on either eye/The President came by.' I am also informed that the Beatles referred to the custom in a song called 'Taxman'. I have no idea where the phrase originated. The ancient Greeks used to place a coin (*naulum,* from *naus,* a ship) in a dead person's mouth to pay the fare Charon demanded to ferry him or her across the river Acheron. I suppose that the custom of placing two pennies on the dead person's eyes superseded the older custom, but when, and why, and where did it happen first?

There are many towns in Ireland in which a street or a building is called The Shambles, and Margaret Gannon from Dublin 3 would like to know the origin of the term. She is aware that the shambles in her home town (she doesn't say where that is) was once a slaughterhouse. The word shamble is as old as the 14th century, and it meant the table on which vendors displayed meat. The word comes from Old English *sceamel,* stool, from Late Latin *scamellum,* a small bench, from Latin *scamnum,* stool. Slaughterhouses came to be known as shambles in the late Middle Ages and it is obvious how sentences such as 'the room was a shambles after the party' came into being. It is thought that the verb *to shamble,* to walk with an awkward or unsteady gait, came from the crudely formed legs of the butcher's *shamble* or earlier *sceamel*.

Finally, a query from Bob Murphy, of Cork city. He wants to know the origin of the phrase 'Bob's your uncle'. It came, Bob, from the nepotistic choice of Tory leader Robert Cecil of his nephew, Arthur Balfour, as Chief Secretary for Ireland in 1900, a most unpopular and surprising choice. My information comes from Jonathon Green's excellent *Dictionary of Contemporary Slang* (Pan Books.)

In Search of Purity

The French are a very serious people when it comes to maintaining the purity of their language. M. Mitterrand declared in 1986 that France was engaged in war with the Anglo-Saxon. They have a law against the encroachment of foreign words since 1911. In 1975 they passed a new Law for the Maintenance of the Purity of the French Language, enabling the government to fine people who used illegal *anglicismes*. Since then they have let loose another watchdog, the Commissariat Général de la Langue française, and have banned jet plane (now *avion à réaction)*, ham–burger (now *steak haché*) and chewing gum (now *pâte à marcher*). Banished too are *le snob* and *le self-made man*, first borrowed over 100 years ago; *ouest* (west), in use for over 700 years; and *rostbif* common enough 350 years ago. It has been suggested that what really rankles the French is not that they are borrowing too many words from foreign languages, but that the rest of the world is no longer borrowing from them. *Le Monde,* once prosecuted for using a forbidden word, sarcastically suggested that 'sandwich' should be rendered *deux morceaux de pain avec quelque chose au mileu*—two pieces of bread with something in the middle. A splendid book called *The Mother Tongue*, by American sociolinguists Bryson and Morrow (New York, 1990) reveals that between 1977 and 1987 no fewer than 40 prosecutions were entered against abusers of the French language; but it may please you to know that the government has conceded defeat on *gadget, hold-up, weekend, blue jeans, self-service, manager,* and *marketing*.

Well, if the French are reticent about borrowing, the Japanese, according to Bryson and Morrow, are devouring English. *Erebata* is elevator; *nekulai* is necktie, *bata* is butter; *sarada* is salad; *remon* is lemon; *chiizu* is cheese; *shyanpu setto* is shampoo and set; *sumato* is smart; *nyuu ritchi* is newly rich; *gurma foto* is glamour photo; *rushawa* is rush hour; *sebiro* is suit of clothes—a corruption of Saville Row; *haikurasu* is highclass; *kyapitaru gein* is capital gain.

Germans nowadays speak of *die Teenagers* and *das Walkout*,—the Ukranians have transformed haircut into *herkot; the* Poles have *ajskrym* for ice cream; but the Italians take the biscuit with their *schiacchenze*—shake hands. At least they didn't make the French mistake of often giving English words entirely contrary meanings. An egghead to the French is an idiot; a jerk, an accomplished dancer.

Newfoundland English

'Newfoundland is a fine plantation. It will be my station until I die,' wrote Donncha Rua Mac Conmara, 18th-century poet and schoolmaster of Co. Waterford, and sometime emigrant to Talamh an Éisc—not the land of fish, by the way, but the fishing ground. A rich fishing ground it was, and in the 18th century a great tide of emigration flowed towards it from the south-east of Ireland. Some fished and came back with their cargoes of salted cod; others remained, and their descendants speak an English reminiscent in terms of both accent and vocabulary, of the English spoken today in Waterford and Ross, Carrick-on-Suir and Dungarvan.

A few years back the University of Toronto Press published a remarkable *Dictionary of Newfoundland English* written by three Memorial University men, G.M. Story, W.J. Kirwan and J.D.A. Widdowson. Let me give you a few of the words they found in their net:

Scrod, noun, applied to a very small article or to a small man. Dinneen has *scráidín,* small portion or article of food—small herring.

Scrawb, noun and verb, scrape. Irish *scrábaim,* I scrape. 'If my name's on that petition, scrawb me off,' a St John's man said.

Sleeveen, noun and verb. In Newfoundland, as in Ireland, a sly, obsequious, deceitful person (Irish, *slíbhín*). 'He's a real sleeveen that fella. He'd steal the two eyes out of your head.' Note the peculiarly Irish idiom, the *two* eyes—an dá shúil.

Sleeveen, verb, means to steal, purloin. 'I'm sure someone sleeveened a rabbit out of that slip.'

Ramlatch, verb, 'to talk meaninglessly and incoherently' is a close relative of *rámáis* and *ráiméis.*

Ral, noun, a rowdy. Irish *raille,* vagabond, trickster. The St John's *Evening Telegraph* reported recently, 'Notwithstanding the number of his assailants he arrested one of them, a notorious ral.'

Skiver, noun, is a word I haven't heard since my schooldays. In both Ross (no Wexfordman worth a Newfoundland herring would call it *New* Ross) and St John's, the word means both a thin person and a small child.

Doone, doonaneen, doonee. Epithet for a member of a group of settlers, originally from Kilkenny. By 1895 the *Tipperary Clear Airs,* the *Waterford Whey Bellies* and the *Cork Dadyeens* were arrayed against the *Yellow Belly* faction, comprised of the *Doones* or *Kilkenny boys,* and the *Wexford Yellow Bellies.* There is a *Yellow Belly Corner* in Water Street in St John's.

Vivent les nôtres!

Clips and Rhyming Doublets

I wonder whether young people in east Kilkenny and south Carlow still *clip*? I don't mean *clip* as used in, let us say, 'a clip in the ear' (cf. Irish *clipeadh*); the clipping I have in mind is a far more pleasing contact, prevalent in my young days in the valleys of the Barrow and the Nore.

Clip, meaning embrace, is old and honourable, certainly as old as Chaucer. The Tudors were very fond of the word. Octavius says over the body of Cleopatra:

> She shall be buried by her Antony.
> No grave upon the earth shall clip in it
> A pair so famous.

Antony himself, a clipper of note, told his soldiers:

> Enter the city, clip your wives and friends,
> Tell them your feats, whilst they with joyful tears
> Wash the congealment from your wounds and kiss
> The honoured gashes whole.

The lexicographer Ivor Brown recorded the word in the fell country of the North of England; it was also recorded in the Glens of Antrim 25 years ago. Where in Ireland do they still *clip*, I wonder?

How are your rhyming doublets and your rhyming alliterative doublets this morning? You know, things like *plinc pleainc*, straight talking; or *longar langar*, complete confusion, known among Irish speakers; *hanky panky*, *crinkum crankum* etc. in common use in English speech.

The late Donagh MacDonagh heard *crinkum crankum* used as a noun among God's Gentry. They told him that it meant anything very gaudy, such as an over-decorated caravan. Ivor Brown heard it used in England in the Irish travellers' sense. He also reminds us that it had the earlier meanings of false, poor stuff, and naughtiness.

Crinkum crankum, he says, occurs in an old folk rhyme about *hanky panky*. A lady over-fond of clipping had to confess that she lost her *binkum bankum* because of her *crinkum crankum*.

I wonder did the Irish *princum prancum*, *pruiseach praiseach*, etc, derive from our neighbours' alliterative rhyming doublets? A thesis here for somebody, surely?

Cockney Slang

The speech of Cockneys has been recorded on a grand scale in recent years by knowledgable and enthusiastic amateurs as well as by those who profess the study of language; witty, eloquent and inventive, Cockney is, of its nature, ephemeral and needs constant attention. Perhaps the best book ever written on Cockney speech is Julian Franklyn's *The Cockney,* published in 1953 and revised and republished the following year. Another splendid study is *The Muvver Tongue* by Robert Barltrop and Jim Wolveridge, published in 1980; and I would also recommend very highly A *Concise Dictionary of Slang and Unconventional English,* edited by Paul Beale from Eric Partridge's 1937 classic. Beale's scholarly and massive edition (Routledge, 1991) contains many fascinating Cockney terms, almost all of them contemporary.

The Cockneys, we should remember, invented rhyming slang and are frequently credited with inventing back slang as well, although I think that they should share that particular distinction with tradesmen, who wished to guard their trade secrets, and with gypsies and other nomads who have had to keep to windward of the law in harder times than these.

Yob is East-End back slang for boy (circa 1890); it has now become *yobbo,* as Anglo-Irish *boyo* has become an extension of boy. By the mid-1980s, Beale informs us, '*yobbo* had become the international word for Brit.' East-end butchers are today's dab-hands at back slang. A woman customer is a *namow,* steak is *kaets* (approximate pronunciation, kites); *exobs* are boxes. A secret lingo, not for the *sremotsuc.*

Many words in Cockney rhyming slang are based on the names of real people. Hence *Mick Jagger,* for lager; *George Raft,* draught; *Gregory Peck,* neck; *Mike Bliss,* piss; *Brahms and Liszt,* pissed; *Mick O'Dwyer,* fire. Yes, the bould Mick is in Beale's great book, but I am terribly sorry to have to tell all good Kerry people that the man in question is not the great footballer and team trainer from Waterville. No, alas, the Cockneys' Mick O'Dwyer dates from the end of the last century. I wonder who he was.

Shelta

The revival at the Abbey of Bryan MacMahon's engaging play about the travelling people, *The Honey Spike,* led me to the pages of the prestigious journal of The Folklore of Ireland Society', *Béaloideas,* to search for information about their secret language, *minkers thawrie,* or *Shelta.* All of 62 years ago, Pádraig Mac Gréine, a national teacher in Ballinalee, Co. Longford, contributed some very valuable articles to the journal, based on information' he had collected from the MacDonough, Power and Collins families.

Mr Mac Gréine tells us that the real experts in this cant were the tinsmiths; but intermarriage with hawkers and horse traders ensured its survival when the craft of tin-smithing died out. It is still in use among travellers; a friend of mine, Mrs Wall, who lives in one of the old horse-drawn caravans, rattles it off to her daughter at such a rate that I suspect that it is, for her at least, almost a complete linguistic system.

The proper pronunciation of Shelta may be obtained, Mr Mac Gréine tells us, by reading the words as if reading Irish. Indeed Irish seems to be basis for many Shelta words, as it is for stonemasons' cant.

The travellers have their own forms of many Christian names. Patrick— *Stoffirt;* John—*Gisán;* Thomas—*Mútas;* Michael—*Srikel;* Martin—*Sartin;* Brigid—*Ribin;* Winifred—*Grúitín;* Mary—*Sraní,* Catherine—*Sraterine.*

Drunk is *sciméis;* laughing, *raiglin;* crying, *lúgin;* married, *lospí;* pin, *nimpin;* ring, *gráinne;* gun, *nuggus;* jail, *rispún;* cart, *lorc;* town, *oura;* helm, *grag;* shop, *opagró, shovie, gruppa;* lodging, *stall, nadas;* day, *tálosc;* night, *dolimi, darahóig;* morning, *hawrum;* tonight, *a chunsk;* good, *buri;* bad, *gami;* big, *tóm;* small, *bini;* door, *rodus;* church, *grépéil;* God, *Dhálúin,* Mother of God, *naderum of the Dhálúin;* Devil, *midil;* father, *gátera;* son, *cam;* sister, *siskár, suicdúir;* brother, *suicár;* grandfather, *lásún gátera;* man, *gleoch, gleoich, feen, gleoinse;* woman, *beóir, mull;* boy, *sam, siblin, sarpóg;* girl, *lakin;* police, *glócotes, shades;* doctor, *sicdúir;* priest, *cúinne;* traveller, *misleoir;* whore, *ripoch.*

Finally, a few phrases to stagger the next traveller who comes to your door. *Lásiúil talosc!*— Good day! *The beoir's at the gruppa* (or *gleoch* as the case may be) and *the beoir* (or *gleoch*) of the *céna* (house) *bucéds the rispa* (wears the trousers). *I'll súni your jeel stoffie!*—I'll see you soon again!

My best wishes to Pádraig Mac Gréine who, I'm glad to hear, is enjoying his retirement in Ballinalee, still driving around to met his friends at the age of 92.

Blowens

Back in the early 60s I first heard the word *blowen.* It was, used by a man who farmed near Cloverfield, in the parish of Kilteely, Co. Limerick. He was a member of the local amateur theatrical company and had rejected some play or other because there were no good parts for *blowens* in it.

Blowen, I was surprised to see, was deemed obsolete by Partridge in 1920. In both Kilteely and Pallasgreen parishes it means a young woman; there is no disrespect to women implied in its use, and in this Limerick has retained what I believe to be the original meaning of a word which by the 17th century had been debased in underworld slang and used along with Natural, Convenient, Tackle, Buttock, Pure, Purest, Pure, to denote 'a mistress or a whore', according to that expert witness Master Thomas Shadwell.

Blowen comes, I think, from the German *blühen,* to bloom or blossom. Partridge, in his magnificent *Dictionary of the Underworld,* contends that if *bloss* is taken along with *blowen,* it would appear possible that both words mean a flower: a blossom, a blowing. Hence we get *blowen* meaning simply a girl, a young woman. The word survived in this complimentary form alongside the slang and cant debasement down through the centuries. Francis Grose, in his *A Classical Dictionary of the Vulgar Tongue* (1785) gives *blowen* as both 'a girl' and 'as mistress or whore of a gentleman of the scamp' (highwayman). Byron, in Don Juan, spelt it *blowing*, and to him the word meant a mistress. Humphrey Potter's 1796 *Dictionary* defines *blowen* as a female shoplifter; while in the young United States a man's *blowen* was his wife.

An interesting cant expression that has become part of ordinary speech in many places Ireland is *to cooper,* meaning to spoil by some imprudent act. A man who has foolishly given away a penalty may be said to have *coopered* his team. *To cooper,* in itinerants' cant, means to mark a house with a sign to show that no welcome can be expected there due to the misdemeanour of some previous traveller. The secret sign is an international one: a triangle with its apex pointing towards the ground. Mayhew mentions it in *London Labour and the London Poor* (1851). As to the expression's origin, I've never seen an explanation that satisfied me.

Parlyaree

An aspect of lexicography which has been rather neglected, I regret to say, is the secret language of the actors and actresses of the old days, when the fit-ups were in vogue and employment much more difficulf to obtain than is the case nowadays. Many years ago some of the older members of RTE's repertory company gave me many and words and phrases, and yes, I've managed to lose them.

I remember that afternoon's talk about the old cant arose from an argument about the origin of *greenroom,* the actors' rest room. Somebody suggested that as greengage, later shortened to green, was late 19th-century theatrical rhyming slang for stage, greenroom had to be stageroom. An interesting hypothesis, but not correct, according to the best dictionaries; Collins for instance, says that greenroom dates from the 18th century, and was probably named from its original colour.

At any rate, Beale gives the Italianate lingua franca of English actors as *parlyaree,* and it has certainly been in vogue since the 18th century. *Parlyaree* comes from the Italian *pargliare,* to speak; by the mid-19th century, when it also became the property of costermongers, it was known also as *parlary* and *palarey.*

There are very interseting accounts of this speech in Beale's *Here There and Everywhere* (1969) and in Sydney Lester's *Vardi the Palarey* (1937). *Vardi* means know. Lester gives the old, pre-decimal coins thus: halfpenny, *medza;* a penny, *soldi;* threepence, *tray-bit;* sixpence, *say soldi;* a shilling, *bionk;* a florin, *dewey bionk;* a halfcrown, *medza caroon;* five shillings, *caroon;* ten shillings,

daiture bionk or *medza funt*; a pound, *funt*. Lester gives the numerals as *una,*
dewey, tray, quattro, chi(n)qua, say, setta, otta, nobba, daiture, lepta, kenza. Only
daiture, kenza and *lepta* are of non-Italian origin. Nobody seems to know
where they originated: I wonder are they Romany words?

The question must be asked, was this the lingua franca of the great actors
and actresses, or was it confined to showmen and to itinerant troupers? It is
generally agreed that until the mid-1850s, it was widely used and it would
appear that the fit-up actors, at least, continued to use it until our own day.
Indeed *parlary* may still be alive and kicking for all I know. Perhaps some of
the old hands would be kind enough to write and enlighten me.

Racist Terms

No doubt you have read that some Americans of Welsh descent have taken
legal action against such empires as the *Los Angeles Times, Newsweek*, the *Wall*
Street Journal and NBC Television. The trouble is over the use of a verb, *to*
welsh, defined by Collins as 'to fail to fulfil an obligation'. The Welsh-Ameri-
can plaintiffs say that to use the verb welsh is as racist as calling a black person
a 'nigger'.

It is widely rumoured that some American judges are well-read, literate
chaps, and I hope that the defendants mentioned above are fortunate in their
arbiter. The controversial word is according to Collins of unknown origin,
and is always spelled with a small *w*. It is as often as not spelled *welch*, and it
was racecourse slang in the 19th century when it meant to pass on counterfeit
money. It is interesting that in current American usage it means to pass on
information to the police. Slang and cant etymologies are notoriously
difficult. The connection with the Welsh nation is, as far as this judge is
concerned, unproven.

The case is an important one; its outcome may well cause a spate of legal
actions against the publishers of dictionaries. Will the unfortunate Dutch sue
over the inclusion of *Dutch courage,* a courage induced by drink, coined in
the 17th century it the height of trade rivalry with Britain; *Dutch uncle,* one
who lays down the law; *Dutch treat,* in which one pays for one's own share
of a meal; not to mention the witty homosexual slang phrases *Dutch*
dumplings, buttocks, and *Dutch girl,* punning on the dikes of Holland? Will
the English sue the French over *le vice anglais*?

I hope not, because dictionaries should be as comprehensive as possible
and not guardians of the high moral ground. As long as words, whether
offensive or not, are, or were, *in common use,* they should be included. I take
exception to patently absurd definitions. Trinity's Bedell Stanford pointed
out the despicable insult to two great nations in the Oxford Dictionary's
definition of *Greek.* 'A cunning or wily person; a cheat, sharper, especially

at cards . . . a person of loose habits . . . an Irishman'. Stanford pointed out
that Dinneen, on the other hand, defined *Gréagach* as 'bright, grand, splendid,
cheerful; an epithet for Ireland's most illustrious Norman-Irish family, the
FitzGeralds' (from the supposed Greek ancestry of the Gherardini). Oxford
has never recanted.

Mots and Sooty Blowens

A letter from a Pallasgreen Co. Limerick man who now lives 'in exile' in
Dublin tells me that the word *blowen* can still be heard in Limerick city. In
a recent conversation in a public house there he heard somebody described
as a *sooty blowen,* meaning a dark-haired girl. He also confirms that *blowen* is
not used in a disparaging sense in Limerick, and that the young woman
referred to would think the term *sooty blowen* complimentary. And why
wouldn't she? Isn't it lovely! Thank you, Mr Ryan.

Miss Hazel West from Belfast takes me to task for not mentioning the
twangman's *mot* in a recent column. 'I fear,' she writes, 'that this word,
obviously a vulgar Dublin pronunciation of *moth*, is doomed to live on in its
present seedy garb'. *Mot,* I'm afraid, has nothing to do with *moth*, no more
than it has anything to do with the Irish phrase *cailín maith*, as another reader
suggested!

Mot is to be found in all the great dictionaries of the language of the
underworld. Francis Grose's *Classical Dictionary of the Vulgar Tongue* (1785)
says that *mot* is cant for 'a woman, a thief's wench, a whore'. The word is
also found in a song printed in London in 1773: it has the intriguing title *The
New Fol de Rol Tit*. Our anonymous poet wrote: 'The first time I saw a
Flaming Mot/ Was at the sign of the Porter Pot.' The lady was on the game.
Jon Bee's *Dictionary of Slang* (1823) says that the word means 'a young woman,
desirable as a sweet-heart', which is the current Dublin meaning of the word.
Curiously, the American *mot* was never anything but 'any decent female,
generally a mother, or sister, or wife', according to *The Ladies' Repository*
(1848) in spite of its title, a book about American underworld language.

Many lexicographers have connected *mot* with *mort*, another old (16th
century or earlier) cant word meaning a criminal's woman. Partridge was, I
think, mistaken in a tentative submission that *mot* was *mort* in disguise. Some
disguise! Jules Manchon, in *Le Slang* (1923), was the first, I believe, to trace
both words to middle Dutch slang *mot,* a prostitute. *Mot-huys* was a brothel.
Partridge has *mot cart*, a vehicle kept for the use of a *dame de compagnie* (19th
century) and *mot case* (20th century) from Dutch *mott-kast*, a brothel. He said,
in his *Dictionary of the Underworld* (1950), that *mot* was by then obsolete
everywhere. He should have asked around Dublin.

Dublin Slang from 1788

I return to a Balbriggan lady's query about the 18th-century cant words in
The Night Afore Larry Was Stretched and other Dublin songs. The scribe Muris
O Gormáin preserved three of these songs for us and my correspondent can
see them in MS G482 in the National Library. The scribe tells us that they
'were quite the Ton with the Inhabitants of Dublin in the year 1788'. Larry,
whose real name was Frederick Lambert, was hanged for murder in 1788
and according to Widdess's *History of the Royal College of Surgeons,* the College
declined to accept his body on the grounds that 'Government has not yet
enabled us to procure an Hall for Publick Dissection'. But to the lady's query:

The *bait* they brought Larry, was food. The nine *glims* in his cell were
lanterns, not candles. *Trap-case*—condemned cell; *case*—house. *Daddle*—
hand. *Claret*—blood. *Nubbling chit*— the gallows; nubbling was hanging, chit
was a variant of *cheat, chet,* meaning 'thing'. *Ground sweat*—a grave. *At darky*
was a Dublin variant of the lovely cant word *darkmans* (singular, note). Joyce
has it in *Ulysses*. 'Fumbally's lane that night; the tanyard smells.

> White thy fambles, (*hands*) red thy gan (*mouth*)
> And thy quarrons (*body*) dainty is.
> Couch a hogshead (*lie down and sleep*) with me, then.
> In the darkmans clip (*embrace*) and kiss.'

I am indebted to Dr J.B. Lyons, medical historian and Joycean, for
identifying the source of the quatrain for me. It is *The Rogue's Delight in Praise
of His Strollinge Mort,* printed in Richard Head's *The Canting Academy,*
London 1673. The suffix, *mans,* comes from the Latin *mens,* through the
ablative *mente,* 'with a mind, intention, mood', according to Partridge.

As for the second song mentioned by my correspondent, *Luke Caffrey's
Kilmainham Minit,* the title refers, I think, not to the length of time it took
the poor man to die, but to his movements at the rope's end: *minit* was cant
for dance—*ex minuet?* The London equivalent was *The Paddington Frisk*:
Tyburn was in that parish. This song is about a failed attempt to revive Mr
Caffrey by injecting whiskey into his jugular. It is a treasury of Dublin
low-life gab in the age of Grattan and Burke.

Jacks and Loo

A lady who tells me that her gentle upbringing precludes her from giving
me either her name or her address wants to know the origin of the words
jacks, jakes, and *loo.* Her Collins, she says, does not have *jacks,* and she wonders
whether the word is an Irish version of *jakes.*

Both words are undoubtedly a variant of the French *Jacques,* and both words were used in 16th century England. Who Jacques was I have no idea. I mentioned the lady's query to the distinguished German philologist, Prof. Manfred Görlach when he visited Dublin recently and he gave me an amusing quotation from a tract by Harrington, dated 1596: 'There was a very tall and serviceable gentleman, sometime Lieutenant of the ordinance, called *M. Jacques Wingfield,* who coming one day, either of business, or of kindnesses to visit a great Ladie in the Court; the Ladie, bad her Gentlewoman aske, which of the Wingfields it was; he told her *Jacques Wingfield;* the modest gentlewoman, that was not so well seene in the French, to know that *Iaques,* was but *James* in English, was so bashfoole, that to mend the matter (as she thought) she brought her Ladie word, not without blushing, that it was M Priuie Wingfield; at which, I suppose the Lady then, I am sure the Gentleman after, as long as he liued, was wont to make a great sport.'

As for *loo,* the lexicographers have had a great sport with this one. Collins suggests that it comes from the French *lieux d'aisance,* places of ease. Partridge's first suggested etymology was from *l'eau;* he later suggested *gardyloo!* a warning the gurriers of Scottish towns learned in some mysterious fashion from their Parisian counterparts (*gare à l'eau!*—beware the water!) and shouted before emptying their chamber pots onto the street below; he finally he came up with: 'far more probably suggested by Waterloo station in London.' He wasn't too sure, was he?

Then there is the *bordalou* theory. This handy object was carried in their muffs by ladies of quality in the 18th century. Shaped like a sauce-boat it was designed by a fashionable Jesuit preacher called Louis Bourdaloue, and used by ladies in difficulty at the opera or while travelling. Others say that *loo* is cognate with *leeward,* for obvious reasons the side a man would use on board ship. And finally, what about Beale's suggestion that loo might simply be an anglicised *lieu,* 'the place'?

Skoolyunes and Snobs

This little column is for people who love the sound and shape of words, including those racy, full-blooded dialect words not commonly given the sanction of lexicography.

Let us start with one of these. The word is *skoolyune*—and that is my own spelling of it for I have never seen it written. As far as I am aware it is to be found only in south east Wexford, in the baronies of Forth and Bargy. A *skoolyune* is a rough apron, what people in some other parts call a bag-apron; and it derives from the Old French (which should surprise nobody who knows anything about the linguistic history of the south east). An *escouillon,* or *escouvillon*, was a swab or a cloth (*escouve*, a broom; Latin *scopa*)—the origin of our Irish *scuab*, of course, and of *scullion*.

Skoolyunes are not worn by *snobs*, possibly, but undoubtedly they used to be. The origin of the word snob is obscure but few words have been turned bun-os-cionn more completely since it began life as 'a shoemaker or cobbler; a cobbler's apprentice' (OED). In this context it appears first in Hone's 'Everyday Book' (1781), where a certain knight is referred to as 'a snob by trade'. Thereafter Cambridge university adopted it. Anybody not a gownsman was called a snob; 'a person belonging to the lower ranks of society, having no pretensions to rank or gentily', as one man put it. Then for some reason it became exactly the opposite, a person admiring, apeing and pretending to gentility.

The word is still used in its original meaning by some of the older people in parts of Wicklow; and only last year a traveller who was camped near Kilpedder told me that he could still make a few shillings on the side 'snobbing'.

It's and Its

Eoin McKiernan writing to the editor of the *Irish Times* from Minnesota, refers to a frequent transgression on the part of journalists and HM's government officials in misspelling the possessive *its*, and suggests that I should say something about the matter.

It was inevitable, I suppose, that the possessive of nouns (*rose's, woman's*) should eventually lead to the analogical form *it's* for the possessive of *it*; and we should, I think, forgive the occasional slip on the part of those who use the apostrophe when we remember that *it's* was the usual spelling down to about 1800. It was the logical way of spelling the word; the 19th-century grammarians—dare I say it?—made a hames of things, and decreed that *its* was the correct way with *it's* reserved as a contraction of *it is*.

It took a long time for *it's* (or *its*, as we now write it) to be regarded as correct. *His* held sway until the middle of the 17th century. Thus Portia: *How far that little candle throws his beams,* and the Bibical *if the salt has lost his savour.* Very often *it* was used as a possessive to avoid the use of *his*, as when Horatio says of the Ghost in *Hamlet, It lifted up it head*, or when the Fool in *Lear* say: 'The hedge sparrow fed the cuckoo so long,/That it had it head bit off by it young.'

The was also used in place of the pronoun: Holland's *Pliny* (1601) has *growing of the own accord.* In this context both *it* and *the* are as old as the 14th century. As the excellent *History of the English Language* by Baugh and Cable (4th ed. Routledge paperback, still in print) points out, *its* was considered by the great Tudors to be a neologism not yet admitted to good use; it is not found in any of the plays of Shakespeare printed during his lifetime, and neither is it in the 1611 Bible. It appears only three times in all of Milton's poetry (Milton died in 1674) but by the end of Dryden's days (he died in 1700) *his* was considered an archaism worthy of comment.

Who can claim the laurels for giving us the useful *its*? It first appeared in print (as *it's*, of course) in 1597, in Nicholas Yonge's *The Second Book of Madrigals*, but no doubt it had been in use in dialect speech before that. Isn't it strange that Shakespeare, Marlowe and the rest had no use for it?

Brats and the Waterford Uvular R

The word *brat*, still in common use all over Britain and Ireland, was recently the subject of a brace of letters to the editor of the *Irish Times*. Its etymology is interesting, especially to us in Ireland, because ultimately it may be of Irish origin. This is what Collins has to say about the word: '*Brat* n., a child, especially one who is dirty or unruly; used contemptuously or playfully, 16th C. perhaps special use of earlier *brat, rag,* from Old English *bratt,* a cloak, of Celtic origin; related to Old Irish *bratt,* cloth.'

The semantic transition is, of course, afforded by a child's clothing. I have never heard the word used to describe a love-child, as one of the editor's correspondents has. The English Dialect Dictionary reminds us of a line of Gascoigne's (in *De Profundis,* 1575): 'O Abrahams brattes, O broode of blessed seede', while Shakespeare has 'To draw the brats of Clarence out of sight', in *Richard the Third.*

The older meaning survives in dialect. *Brat* can mean a child's pinafore, a rag, a nappy, a large course apron used by factory workers and sheep shearers, and in contemporary Glasgow slang, a condom. In Ayrshire, as in Rhymer Rab's day, itinerant harvest workers ask for *bite and brat*—food and clothing in return for their labour. Donegal sheep men put a *brat* on a ewe's hind quarters to prevent her being covered by the ram. Brat is sometimes used in Ireland as a contemptuous word for a child born out of wedlock. The archivist, Mrs Eilish Ellis, found the word, denoting illegitimacy, in the pre-1845 Parish Registers of Tynagh, Co. Galway.

A Cork reader wants to know where the people of Waterford and south Kilkenny got their distinctive uvular R, produced by the vibration of the uvula, imitated with glee by frustrated Wexford hurling fans, and to perfection by Mr Niall Tóibín. Could it be a Norman importation, my correspondent asks, as it is identical to the French uvular R.

No, it is not of Norman origin. The French uvular R is a comparatively modern Parisian development. It had become general in Parisian speech by the beginning of the 19th century; it became fashionable in the military academies and was widely imitated north of the capital. The south held out against it; the medieval linguo-dental *r* still predominates among southern rugby players, I've noticed.

Where did the Kilkenny and Waterford people get their 'Parisian' R? I haven't the faintest idea, I'm sorry to say.

Phil Wall's Words

Phil Wall from the parish of Our Lady's Island, near Carne in Co. Wexford, was ninety when I first met him back in the late sixties. He was well aware of the richness of his Forth English, and he used many words whose original meaning have long since changed in other places. I remember him shaking his stick one day at a *spiritogue* of a child of about four who was playing dangerously close to the edge of the pier; the child's mother was told gently to wake up and have a care for her little *oaf*. That word, *oaf*, now used exclusively to define a dolt or a half-wit, was in common use up to the seventeenth century with the meaning sprite, goblin, or elf. Indeed it shares a common etymology with *elf*, ultimately Indo-European *albho*, white, which eventually gave Old English *ælf* and Old Norse *alfr*, elf goblin, and then English *elf*. Variant forms also survived, and Shakespeare has *aulfe, aufe* and *ouph* as well as *oph* and *oaf*, but with the new meaning, bumbling fool, simpleton. So, where Shakespeare changed with the times, Phil Wall did not.

Phil was interested in nautical words and phrases, and perhaps the dictionaries which run up the 'of unknown origin' flag after the term *fly-by-night*, meaning brief, permanent, untrustworthy, would be interested to know that he said that in the days of the old schooners the *fly-by-night* was a big square sail used on a reach (sailing on a tack with the wind on or near abeam). It was easy to handle and easy to set, and could be taken in quickly and easily in the darkness. The other heavier sail was replaced at dawn.

As we listened in the Lobster Pot in Carne one night to a musician playing a well-known tune called *The Lady's Pantalettes*, Mr Wall asked me did I know how the tune got its name. I had to profess ignorance. The item in question, he said, was often carried instead of a skyscraper, a triangular sail of very thin canvas, or the moonraker, an equally thin square sail, set merely for show above the skysails. The old wind-jammer men regarded the lady's pantalettes as a good luck charm, and neither the divil nor Dr Foster could persuade them to lower them!

Kim-Kam

I must thank an anonymous reader for sending me approximately 300 rare words collected by the late Donagh MacDonagh, that are not, as I first suspected, part of the vocabulary of the travelling people. One among them took my fancy immediately. You won't find it in the standard dictionaries, neither is it in any of the glossaries of shelta, romany, slang or cant that I've looked at. I had given up hope of ever finding the word in print when I came across it in a little book by the late Ivor Brown, the Scottish lexicographer, which I picked up on the Dublin quays many years ago. The word, or compound is *kim-kam* and it is an alliterative doublet with no international pedigree. Brown says that it was in its heyday in the 17th century, and that it did not, as far as he knew, travel north across the Scottish border. It means what *agley* meant to Burns; the best laid schemes of ourselves and the mice went *kim-kam* south of the border, and on this side of the Irish Sea, too, it would seem.

Brown relates how that admirable gossip, John Aubrey, while recording his own 'accidents', as he termed them, of a disturbed life, describes the very bad time he had in 1664. He had a 'terrible fit of the spleen and piles' in Orleans, came home, fell off his horse near an inn (coming or going?) and suffered 'damage which was like to have been fatall. This year all my affaires ran *kim-kam*. Made my first addresses in an ill-houre to Joane Sumner. Arrested in Chancery Lane, at Mrs Sumner's suite'. *Kim-kam* indeed, but better news followed. 'Triall with her at Sarum. Victory and six hundred pounds dammage, though devilish opposition against me!'

What this was all about he doesn't explain, but we may guess. Sadly, we know little about Aubrey, beyond his autobiography of ill-houres and *kim-kam*. We know little of *kim kam* either, so, should the donor of MacDonagh's words know where he collected them, perhaps he or she would be good enough to get in touch with me.

Mrs Dympha Moore of Cahir; James Lundon of Tirellan Heights, Galway; Críostóir Gallagher of New Inn, Cashel, and Roger Ackerley of Carranroo, Co. Clare, have all pointed out to me that the second element in the compound *kim-kam* may be none other than our own Irish *cam*, crooked, bent. Mr Ackerley quotes Partridge as saying that the compound *clean-kam* was used by Shakespeare; sure enough the glossary at the back of my Alexander Text has *kam* meaning contrary, and led me to this little exchange in Corolianus:

Silinius Velutus: This is clean kam.

Brutus: Merely awry.

If *kam* is borrowed from Irish, where does *kim* come from? I don't think, with due respect to Partirdge, that it is related to clean, which Shakespeare would have pronounced clane. But it is interesting that clean/clane is still widely used in Ireland as an intensifier. Last night I heard a man suggesting that a certain politician was 'clane mad'. Mr Lundon, an east-Limerick man by birth, tells me that John Aubrey's *kim-kam* was in his part of the world known as a *conjafrey*. I wonder where that came from.

Remembering Prayers

A lady from Bangor, Co. Down, would like to know if what Sam Hanna Bell called *remembering prayers* are, or ever were, said in the deep South. These were not prayers for the repose of the souls of the dead, she tells me, but short prayers of an intercessory nature, usually composed *ex tempore*: 'the kind of prayers parents might say for their children in time of sickness, or that the children might say for the recovery of a lost pet'. No, I've never come across *remembering prayers*, nor have I been able to find a reference to them in any of the Anglo-Irish glossaries; but Wright's *English Dialect Dictionary* mentions them, and they are given a Scottish provenance, from the Burns country, in fact. Galt's *Provost* (1822), has: 'During the remembering prayer, Mr Pittle put up a few words for criminals under sentence of death.' Whether the term is still used in Ayrshire I'm afraid I don't know.

My correspondent's letter reminded me of a usage of the word *remember* I have frequently noted in Counties Wexford and Wicklow; and for all I know it may be found in other places as well. A man told me once that I remembered him of my mother's people. Recently a traveller to whom I had promised a recording of her kinsman, the Wexford piper Felix Doran, told me that she'd call again 'to remember me about it'. The English Dialect Dictionary gives us many examples of this usage from England, the oldest being from 1790, and recorded in the North Country: 'If you will remember me of it'. In Yorkshire they say 'an ye be remembered', meaning, if you remember.

Omlish and Alfratch

A lady from Kilmacthomas, Co. Waterford, has sent me a very interesting word indeed. 'Here in mid-Waterford', she writes, 'the children at Hallowe'en go out in the *omlish*, the modern trick-or-treat. The word *omlish* is not known either in east or west Waterford'.

My correspondent is probably right in claiming this word for mid-Waterford, but what is its origin? The redoubtable Dinneen gives us our first clue. He has: '*alamuis*, excitement, merrymaking extravagance; *alamuis cainte*, wild extravagant talk; dainties got on Hallowe'en; *oíche alamuis(e)*, a name for Oíche Shamhna in Waterford.' So far so good; *alamuis* becomes *omlish* through metathesis, the transposition of two sounds or letters in a word. But is the word of Irish origin or is it a borrowing? My friend, Dr Nicholas Williams, has convinced me that a borrowing it is. He says that *omlish/alainuis/* is simply *Hallowmass* in disguise, a word used as far back as the 14th century for the feast of All Saints.

Alfratch is also found on the lips of rural Waterford people, but the query concerning it comes from Mr J. Murray of Macroom, Co. Cork. Written *alfraits* in Irish, it means 'a scoundrel, a rascal', according to Ó Dónaill's dictionary; Dinneen goes a little further saying that *alfraits* is 'a scold, a barge, a man of rude manners at table, a peevish child'. The word's origin troubles my correspondent who gives us a clue in his spelling of the word. Dinneen also noticed that the word's termination was pronounced like the English— *atch*, and came to the conclusion that *alfraits* was simply *old fratch*. He was right, as usual. The English Dialect Dictionary gives *fratch* as 'a rude, quarrelsome person; a playful child'; it is still common in England's north country, as is the verb. 'Them at will interfere between man an wife at's fratchin', is a Yorkshire saying. Now that I come to think of it, the first and only time I heard the word *fratch* was in a Co. Wexford stable, when a Yorkshire horse dealer started his negotiations in time-honoured fashion, with an insult, calling a horse he wanted to buy 'a bit of a fratch'. He went on to fork out thirty grand for him.

By Hook or by Crook

A woman from Fethard in Co. Wexford asks me to solve a problem which she says, has been bothering her for years. A lot of people in her part of the world believe, she says, that the phrase 'by hook or by crook' refers to some old-timer or other—she thinks it may have been Richard the Second— vowing to land among us either by Hook Head or by Crook, another Wexford headland. True or false? she asks.

False, mam, as far as I know. This is William Cobbett in 1822: 'I have always observed that woodland and forest labourers are best off in the main . . . they have a three weeks harvest in April or May; that is to say in the season of barking, which in Hampshire is called *stripping,* and in Sussex *flaying,* which employs women and children as well as men. And then, in the great article of *fuel.*They buy *none.* It is miserable work where this is to be *bought,* and where, as at Salisbury, the poor take by turns the making of fires at their houses to boil four or five tea-kettles. What a winter-life those lead, whose turn it is not to make the fire! At Launceston in Cornwall a man, a tradesman too, told me that the people in general could not afford to have fire in ordinary, and that he himself paid 3d for boiling a leg of mutton at another man's fire! The leather-legged race (the woodsmen) know none of these miseries. They literally get their fuel *by hook or by crook,* whence doubtless comes that old and very expressive saving, which is applied to those cases where people will have a thing by one means or another.'

The phrase was used by both John Wyclif and John Gower, contemporaries of Chaucer, but Will Cobbett, it seems, was on the right track. The old forest laws of England, which gave all the forest lands to the king, also laid down that the common people could enter these lands without permission to remove dead wood from the ground or dead branches from the trees, of the latter, only such branches as could be brought down by hook or by crook. Ivor Brown wrote that in order to satisfy the meaning, 'by fair means or foul', we must assume that the ancient shepherds found an excuse to tend their sheep with crooks that were exceedingly long or unusually heavy.

Whether this is another example of folk etymology I don't know. But most lexicographers are satisfied that of the many explanations offered down the years, this one is the most plausible.

Cummer

That good word *cummer*, also found as *kimmer* has never travelled south of Co. Down as far as I know. The *cummer* can be either a godmother, a gossip, or any woman old enough to marry. The word is, of course, Scots, from old French *commère,* a sponsor at baptism. The English Dialect Dictionary gives us the word *cummerfeall* 'an entertainment formerly given on the recovery of a woman from inlying'.

The Diary of Elizabeth Muir (1714–95), who lived in south-west Scotland, gives a fascinating account of these parties.

'On the forth week after the lady's delivery she is sett on her bed on a low footstool; the bed is covered with some neat piece of sewed work or white sattin, with three pillows at her back; she in full dress with a lapped head dress and a fan in her hand. . . . Toward the end of the week all the friends were asked to what was called the Cummer's feast. This was a supper, where, every gentleman brought a pint of wine to be drunk by him and by his wife. The supper was a ham at the head and a pirimid fowl at bottom. This dish consisted of four or five ducks at bottom, hens above; partrages at tope. There was an eating posset in the middle of the table, with dryed fruits and sweet-meats at the sides. When they had finished their supper the meat was removed, and in a moment everybody fled to the sweetmeats to pocket them. Upon which a scramble insued, chairs overturned and every thing on the table; wrassalling and pulling at one another with the utmost noise. When all was quiet'd they went to the stoups (for there were no bottles) of which the woman had a good share. For tho it was a disgrace to be seen drunk, yet it was none to be a little intoxicate in good company. A few days after this the same company was asked to the Christening, which was allwise in the Church; all in high dress; a number of them young ladys, who were call'd maiden Cummers. One of them presented the Child to the Father. After the Cerrimony they dine and supped togither, and the night often concluded with a ball.'

Was all this revelry in honour of some Scots counterpart of Lucina, the

goddess of childbirth? Does it survive? Did it, like the word *cummer*, transfer
to Ireland? I'd love to know.

That's Cat, Precious

Some weeks ago a reader requested information about the provenance of the
expression *That's cat,* used to describe something unpleasant or queer. I was
about to confess to failure when a letter arrived from J. Callaghan of
Blackrock, which included a piece of considerable interest from a recent issue
of *New Scientist.* I quote: 'Still on Folkstone, our report that the good people
of that town call the Seacat 'the vomit comet' because of its tendency to
lurch around in the water, has prompted a reader to point out that it already
had an admirably appropriate name. According to the *New English Dictionary,*
to cat is: (colloq.) to vomit, verb intrans., to be sick. Hence the maritime
aphorism 'Never cat to windward'.

So, is the *cat* of my schooldays connected with to *cat,* meaning to get sick?
Perhaps it is; and it doesn't bother me that the NED gives cat as a verb. Slang
is notoriously fickle.

Miss Joan Murphy tells me that she heard a strange use of the word *precious*
at the Enniscorthy greyhound track recently. Somebody described a dog as
precious fast. Precious, as an intensifier has been around for a long time, from
the 13th century in fact, and it's still found in a few phrases: *precious little* is
one that comes to mind. But it is perhaps more commonly used in rural
Wexford than in other places. I've heard *precious sexy* there in my ramblings
(not to describe myself, I should add), *precious lovely* and even *precious ugly.*

Precious, from Old *French precios,* from Latin *pretium,* price, value, has
struck hard times. Oliver Cromwell, at his laconic best, wrote to an officer:
'Sir, God hath taken away your oldest son by a cannon shot. It brake his leg.
We were necessitated to have it cut off, whereof he died. Truly he was
exceedingly beloved in the Army of all that knew him. But few knew him
because he was a precious young man, fit for God.' The adjective precious
would now suggest Mercutio's 'antic, lisping, affecting fantasticoes, new
tuners of accents, strange flies, pardonnez-mois', and the old meaning is
nowadays applied only to virtues, jewels and the blood of Christ. Stones may
still be called precious; a dying soldier may not. That's the way of the world
of words.

Archbishop Trench

Richard Chenevix Trench, Archbishop of Dublin, is remembered as a
scholar who did pioneering work in lexicography. It is said of him that he

laced his sermons with so many asides about the origins of the words he used that he sometimes forgot what it was he was preaching about. He was one of a handful of 19th century scholars who made the study of words and their origins immensely popular: one of his books, *On the Study of Words*, ran to 24 editions.

A classicist, he reminded us of the importance of the Latin substratum of English. *Insult*, he pointed out, once meant to jump on (*in* + *saltare*, to jump). He visualised a triumphant soldier jumping on a prostrate enemy. *Succour*, through Old French *sucurir*, came from Latin *succurrere*, to hurry to help, from Latin *sub*, under, and *currere*, to run. He imagined a person running under another to break his fall: a Roman Catcher in the Rye, you might say.

To *exonerate*, to free from blame, once meant to take away a burden, *onus*. Ships were once exonerated; now they are unloaded. To be *examined* once meant to be weighed. This, through Old French *examiner*, from the Latin *examinare*, to weigh, from *examen*, the tongue of a balance, from *exigere*, to thrust out, from *agere*, to thrust. *Supercilious* was born 'because haughtiness with contempt of others expresses itself by the raising of the eyebrows or *supercilium*.

Companion, he reminded his readers is from Late Latin *companio*, literally one who eats bread with another, ultimately from Latin *cum*, with, + *panis*, bread. *Rival* is from another Late Latin word, *rivalis*, literally one who shares the same brook. He speculated that *trivial* may be from the *trivium*, or three preparatory disciplines—grammar, arithmetic and geometry—as distinguished from the four more advanced, or *quadrivium*; these and those together being esteemed in the Middle Ages to constitute a complete liberal education.' But he did not discount the theory that trivial may have come from *tres viae*, three roads, 'and *trivialities* mean such talk as is beholden by those idle loiterers that gather at this meeting of three roads.'

What would Dr Trench think of these our (almost) Classics-less days? Of universities which do not teach his beloved Latin and Greek? O triste plane acerbumque funus!

Waur and Trance

'His bark is waur nor his bite', was a phrase used by the neighbours of Mrs E. Craig in the Coleraine of her youth. She wants to know where the word *waur* came from.

It has been recorded all over Britain, but in Ireland it seems to be confined to those planted districts whose dialects have been strongly influenced by Scots. You'll find it written as *war*, *waur*, *waar*, *wer* and *waure* and it is used as an adjective, adverb, noun and verb. Scott has 'fain to leave the country for fear that waur had come of it' in *Rob Roy*. Watson in his *Border Bards* (1859) has 'The times are aye changing in frae bad to war'; and Burns in *Kirk's Alarm* wrote resignedly, 'She cou'd ca' us nae waur than we are.'

Hence *war-fared* worse looking, *war-hand*, the left hand, and the phrases *war for wear, war side out,* cross, ill-tempered. '*Ill comes upon waur's back*', meaning one misfortune succeeds another, was a phrase known to both Carleton and Peadar O'Donnell. I have heard '*Don't take war*', meaning 'Don't take offence, in the Rosses. Kelly's Scots *Proverbs* (1721) has 'The water will never war the widdie', which means 'He that is born to be hanged will never be drowned.' *Widdie*, by the way is a Scottish child's name for a duckling.

So, Mrs Craig's word is in English since circa 1200, when it was written *werre* in *Ormulum*. It is from the Old Norse *verr,* adverb; *verri*, adjective, worse.

Trance is another interesting word found in the north of our sainted isle. I am grateful to Janet Henderson for it. It was her mother's word for a hall-way and was once common in the Ards peninsula.

This word came from Scotland, where it can also mean a passage within a house, the landing at the top of the stairs, an alley outside a house, a close. Scott has 'he led the way through halls and trances.' In the 1881 edition of *Folk Lore* you'll find 'leaving the kitchen you found yourself in a long passage or trance.' Trance was also used figuratively. Rutherford's wonderful *Letters* of 1660 refers to 'That Lord Jesus, who knoweth the turnings and windings that are in that black trance of death.' Rutherford was *not* alluding to the hypnotic state resembling sleep, although that trance, too, is from the Old French *transe* a passage, ultimately from Latin *transire*, to go over.

Tipperary Words

Some of the ladies who live within a ten mile radius of the hurling stronghold of Toomevara, Co. Tipperary, have a nice line in invective, according to one of their own, who begs anonymity. A word in fairly common use is *soult*, and my correspondence wonders about its origin. She heard the word used to the fiancé of a local girl: 'God help us, but did you see the soult she brought home with her! A real oul' crilly, honest to God.' Ouch.

Soult is the Irish *samhailt*, a spectre of apparition. The word *crilly* I found in an Irish Folklore Commission manuscript from Goold's Cross, dated 1935. Crilly was glossed as 'a shivering sort of person, one who appears to be cold, and bent down with misery.' The schoolmaster's reference to shivering suggests that it is related to *crith*, trembling, or some word like *crith-eagla*, fear causing trembling.

Skyrky is a word I've never come across in the English or Irish, in any form. 'Lord, but she's very skyrky in herself since she came into the bit of the uncle's money', said the Tipperary woman. I'm pretty sure this is from the Irish *scadhrach,* which Dinneen gives as an adjective meaning blatant.

Jane Reid of Bangor, Co. Down, wrote about the word *allegate*, which means to dispute or argue. I came across this word in Jane Barlow's *Idylls* (1892), which I read recently mainly to pillage its store of dialect words, I must confess. She has: 'They'll bicker and allegate over every hand's turn.' I'm told the word is now confined to Ireland, although *allegation*, meaning a dispute or quarrel, is still found in Galloway. Anyway, *allegate* is a by-form of *allege*, to adduce, to bring forward, from the Latin *allegare*.

Finally, an interesting word from Yorkshire, and not at all obsolete, as Oxford would have found out had it consulted the gypsies. The word is *arse-verse* and it doesn't mean a collection of inferior poetry. No, it is a prayer or incantation written on the side of a house (or caravan) to prevent fire. In the old days the verse seems to have been a spell against both fire and witch-craft. Anne James, late of Sligo, she says, sent me the words from York.

The *arse* part is from *ars-*, past participle stem of Latin *ardere*, to burn. It survives in the French and English *arson*.

Moral and Some Donegal Words

A Mayo lady who lives in Dublin asks if I've ever come across a word once common, she tells me, in the north and west of her native county. The word is *moral* and it means the exact likeness, or counterpart.

Because of its use by Carleton, Brooke, and other northern writers, I had never guessed that the word was (is?) common in the west; but sure enough Emily Lawless has it in her novel *Grania* from the Mayo of 1892: 'A fine big girl she was, just the moral of that Grania there.' Carleton has: 'You're the moral of a Methodist preacher.' I myself have heard the word used in Donegal, and I was foolishly searching for an Irish origin until I found that the word is common currency all over Britain. The oldest printed source is Constable's *Sonnets* of 1590, a chap whose political correctness would go down a treat in Teheran: 'Fooles be they that inveigh 'gainst Mahomet, Who's but a morral of love's monarchie.' As to its origin, I can only guess that it is a cognate of *model*, which itself from French *modelle*, from Latin *modulus*, diminutive of *modus*, measure, manner.

From a little further north comes a query as to the origin of *freets*, a word meaning superstitions: anything in the shape of omens, charms, etc. Mary Campbell, who was reared near Glenties, says that the word is very commonly used around the coast, and that sometimes *froots* is heard.

It is usually written *freits*, and is common in Scotland. It is an old word, as old as the *Cursor Mundi* of 1300, where we find: 'folud wiche-crafte and frete, and charmynge.' Traynor's English Dialect of Donegal has it. He says the word comes from the Old Norse *frétt*, news, augury. The EDD hedges its bets. I would hazard Old English *friðian*, to protect, or its Old Norse cousin, *friða*, to restore to peace or personal security, which is what omens and charms and all sorts of pishogues are supposed to do.

Two other words are bothering Mary. One is *mullin*. 'Cows are sent to the mullin in summer.' This is Irish *maoileann*, a brow, a summit, a ridge of a hill. The other word is *freath*, which my correspondent describes as suds, or soapy water. I had to go no further than my own kitchen to find this one, where my informant told me that further north in Donegal *freath* means a quick wash. From Old English *fréopan*, to foam. Related, of course, to our modern *froth*.

All My Eye

Chris Renton is a Yorkshireman who now lives in Blackberry Lane, Delgany, and he recently set me thinking about the phrase 'all in my eye'. An interesting phrase it is.

The first writer to use it was, it seems, Oliver Goldsmith, back in 1768. A common version is 'all my eye, and Betty Martin'. I've heard it in Kilkenny and in south Carlow, and my Yorkshire friend tells me that it is widely used from the dales to the nose of Cornwall.

Many's the man from Grose to Partridge has had fun attempting to figure out who Betty Martin was. Grose, the author of the 1795 *Dictionary of the Vulgar Tongue,* had the phrase. John Bee's *Dictionary of the Turf* (1823), says that the entire phrase is a corruption of *O mihi, beate Martine*, but I wouldn't put my shirt on that particular runner.

In 1914 the Classic scholar L.A. Waddell derived the phrase from *O mihi, Brito Martis*—Oh, (bring help), to me, Brito Martis. The lady in question was the tutelary goddess of Crete, and her cult was associated with the sun-cult of the Phoenicians, who did a roaring trade with the Celts of Cornwall, swapping this-and-that for tin.

It is said that the late Pádraic Óg Ó Conaire, when working on a radio news bulletin, translated 'there was uproar in the Commons today' into an Irish equivalent of they beat the living daylights out of one another. His interesting rendition, as well as proving that one man's uproar is another man's riot, hints at the older meaning of the word: insurrection, tumult, treason, rather than ungentlemanly shouting.

Uproar didn't originate with 'roar'. Its origin is the Dutch *oproer*, literally, up-movement. Tindale and Coverdale were the first to use the English word in their translations of the Bible from Luther's German. Coverdale has, from 2 Kings: 'Athalia rente hir cloths & sayde, vproure. vproure'. Closer to the kind of vproure that Ó Conaire had in mind than to the antics frowned on by Betty Boothroyd. The King James version has 'treason, treason.'

Egg on

A Clontarf reader, Mary O'Brien, would like me to shed some light on the term to *egg on*, to incite. 'Is it American slang?' she asks, 'and which or whether, what is its origin?'

Well, it is certainly in common use in America, as it is on this side of the pond; but don't think we should classify this expression as slang; it has too long a pedigree. *Egg* in this sense is from Old English *eggian*, from Old Norse *eggja*. to urge. It is related to Old English *ecg*, edge, and Middle Low German *eggen*, to harrow. Chaucer has *eggen* to incite, in *The Parsons Tale*. He also has *eggement*, incitement.

Joan Gillespie of Luton wrote to tell me of a word common near the town of sweet Strabane in her youth. The word is *stucker*, and it meant a sponger. Traynor's dictionary of Donegal English has this one under *stuccour*. (His phonetic transcription would suggest 'stooker'). Anyway, his informants gave him the word both as a verb and a noun. '1. v. 'To follow a person in the expectation of getting something. 2. n. A person, who, though uninvited, goes to a place in expectation of something. Also a dog that sits watching a person at meals in expectation of getting food.' The word is the Irish *stocaire*, an interloper or sponger.

Sister M.A. Nic Cárthaigh of the Dominican convent, Cabra, wrote to suggest that the word *moidered*, confused, recently mentioned in this column, might be the Irish *modartha*, which in *The Annals of Ulster* and the *Annals of Loch Cé* had the meanings dark, murky, morose.

The good lady may well be right. The implication that the word travelled to Scotland and northern England in medieval times is plausible; and the fact that *moithered* is found as far south as Kent, Surrey and Dorset, needn't trouble us.

Addle is a word sent to me by J.E. Baird of Belfast. It meant a stagnant, foul-smelling pool, the run-off from a dung-heap. This is another of the many northern farming words imported from Scotland. Burns has it in *Kirk's Alarm*: 'Then lug out your ladle, Deal brimstone like adle, And roar every note of the damned.' It came from Old English, *adela*, foul water. Old Swedish has *adel* in the compound *ko-adel*, cow urine.

Fridgies and Slammicks

During the winter I heard a Scots visitor to my part of the world complaining about the referee in a televised rugby match. He (the ref.) had warned a player for trying to decapitate an opponent in the front row with an upper-cut, but the Scotsman claimed that it was a fidgie, for God's sake.

Fidgie, sometimes *fugie, foodgie*, or *fugee*, is a schoolboy word for a tap, a shove, a light blow. The English Dialect Dictionary, quoting the *Glasgow Herald* of a century ago, has 'In those days, as now, it was not always necessary to follow up a challenge with a blow, but the boy who would not fight another of his size after receiving a fidgie was unanimously voted a coward and generally sent to Coventry. When a fidgie was not sufficient provocation to produce a fight a second blow was often given, and this couplet repeated— 'That's your fidgie, that's your blow; Ye're bet and I'm no.'

Fidgie, in all its forms, has long left the schoolyards of Scotland for the pubs and the playing-pitches, and it has strolled into Scots literature. John Service, the author of *Dr Duguid* (1887) and other engaging works in the Ayrshire tongue, has 'With James it was aye a word and a lick, so by way of fugé he gied Willie a cloor on the haffet.' (*Cloor* is from Old Norse *klor*, a scratching; *haffet* is from Old English *healfheafod*, the front part of the head.)

As to *fidgie's* origin, it's figurative meaning is coward and so is related to *fugitive*, ultimately from Latin *fugere*, to run away.

A Dun Laoghaire reader, Claire Delaney, asks if I can throw light on the word *slammick*, noun, a slovenly person, a word used by an uncle of hers. I'd like to know where this uncle grew up. Ó Dónaill has *slaimice*, meaning an untidy person; a messy eater, a gobbler. A west Cork poitín maker I once knew called his wife a slaimice for knocking a bottle of the nectar off the kitchen table. A native word, so? you may well ask. I doubt it, somehow. The word *slammock* and its numerous variants have been recorded all over Britain. The English Dialect Dictionary glosses it as 'A dirty, untidy person; a slattern, a hulking, lazy, contemptible fellow; an awkward, waddling person or animal.' It also has *slammockin*, noun; 'a dirty, slovenly woman; an ungainly, burly person'.

Words are the divil's own travellers, as the Tailor of Gougane, a neighbour of my poitín maker, once remarked.

Nominy

More than once in this column I have had occasion to refer to Phil Wall of Lady's Island, Co. Wexford, a man who was 90 when I met him in the late sixties. One of the words he used in relation to the local Carne mumming play was *nominy*. To him it meant a mumming rhyme. As far as I am aware the word has now gone from the local speech. I wonder does it survive anywhere in Ireland?

In England it is still in use from Yorkshire to Pembrokeshire. It now means a rigmarole, a longwinded, tiresome speech. It used to mean a mumming rhyme; also a complimentary doggerel used at weddings; and an uncomplimentary doggerel used during the ceremony of riding the stang, a rural punishment for wife/husband beating which comprised of the culprit being carried around tied to a pole, while being pelted with ordure and drenched with buckets of water and worse. Here's a stang nominy from early 19th century Yorkshire: 'With a ran tan tan On my old tin can, Mrs— and her good man, she banged him, she banged him, For spending a penny when he stood in need. She up with her three-footed stool; She struck him so hard, and she cut so deep, Till the blood ran down like a new stuck sheep.'

Poor girls knitting for a living made up their own nominies to relieve the boredom. This is from the Northhampton of the 1880s: 'Needle to needle and stitch to stitch. Pull the old woman out of the ditch. If you ain't out by the time I'm in, I'll rap your knuckles with my knitting pin.'

Phil Wall's nominy represents the Latin *nomine* in the prayer *In nomine Patris* etc., the invocation to the Trinity once used by a Priest before his sermon.

A young travelling woman asked me the other day if I'd mind filling her sookey; the pump at the bottom of the village had gone dry. *Sookey*, kettle, was new to me. I asked her if she had heard the word *tiddrer*. She shook her flaxen head at my ignorance. 'A tiddrer is a taypot, boss, she said. This is a sookey. Men! You don't make tay in the sookey.' 'Shelta?' I asked. Another shake of the head.

Her sookey is found all over rural England, it seems, and a friend has heard it in Carlow. Glad to have the word, I made tay for us both in the tiddrer, which I think is a form, of taydrawer, when sookey sang.

Jimp and Traipse

I have never heard the word *jimp*, slender neat, elegant, and, by extension of the meaning, scarce, south of the border. An Antrim lady, Mary Craig, reminded me of it, and I'm sorry to have to tell her that I don't know its origin, apart from the fact that it is an importation from Scotland. The Lass of Lochroyan enquired. 'O wha will shoe my bonny foot? And wha will bind my middle jimp Wi' a lang, lang linen band?' 'Thy waist sae jump,' wrote Burns in 'Parnassus Hill'. Hence *jimpy*, used by Rhymer Rab to describe Bonie Ann, and by a lesser light, Ballantine, in his *Poems* of 1856: 'Bawbee dolls the fashions apit, Sae rosy cheekit, jimpy shapit,' (A bawbee, by the way, was a Scots coin, the equivalent of an English halfpenny.)

Jimp can also mean scanty; tight; narrow; deficient in quantity. The *Ballymena Observer* of 1892 has 'gimp measure'. Hence the adverb *jimply*, scarcely. 'Jimply a mile from here', wrote Lynn Doyle. *Jimp*, apparently, is as jimply used in England as it is in the south of Ireland. Perhaps some reader can help trace its etymology.

That good word *traipse*, still regarded as slang, is on the mind of M.

Bennett of Dalkey. Dr Johnson described it as 'A low word. To walk in a careless or sluttish manner'; and he mentioned that it was used by Mr Pope. Swift wrote 'I was traipsing to-day with your Mr Sterne'; I think he meant walking carelessly, aimlessly. The meaning seems to have changed ever so slightly since the 18th century. Collins says that to *traipse* is 'to walk heavily or tiredly'.

Traipse is in English since the 16th century. The word is also a noun. We've all heard such sentences as 'It's a tiring traipse up those three flights of stairs'. Often spelled *trapes*, it also meant a slovenly or slatternly woman. Cotton, in 1673 has: 'I had not car'd If Pallas here had been preferr'd; But to bestow it on that Trapes, It mads me.'

As to its origin, the great dictionaries have nothing to offer. Eric Partridge, however, may have solved the problem, although his conclusion was tentative. He thought it was 'perhaps cognate with obsolete *trape* to walk idly to and fro, which probably derives from the medieval Dutch *trappen* to tread'.